THE
MOUSE THAT
SAVED THE WEST

The True and Secret History of How the World Oil Crisis Was Solved by the Duchy of Grand Fenwick . . .

or

THE MOUSE THAT SAVED THE WEST

Leonard Wibberley

WILLIAM MORROW AND COMPANY, INC.

New York   1981

Library of Congress Cataloging in Publication Data

Wibberley, Leonard Patrick O'Connor, 1915–
   The mouse that saved the West.

    I. Title.
PS3573.I2T7   813'.54   80-25567
ISBN 0-688-00364-8

Printed in the United States of America

First Edition

1 2 3 4 5 6 7 8 9 10

BOOK DESIGN BY MICHAEL MAUCERI

I have examined this manuscript thoroughly and affirm that the facts related therein are as accurate as those in any other history I have read.

VINCENT,
Count of Mountjoy

THE CASTLE,

DUCHY OF GRAND FENWICK

THE
MOUSE THAT
SAVED THE WEST

CHAPTER

1

The Count of Mountjoy, deep in thought, was lying on a huge couch in his bedroom in the castle of Grand Fenwick examining the ceiling. The ceiling was decorated in a design of red lions, white unicorns and yellow roses. It was the work of one Derek or Dennis of Pirenne (1400–circa 1467), who had died in some chivalric scuffle with a knight of Vignon over a lady of quality. The exact date of his death seemed to have been deliberately obscured to protect his slayer or some other secret.

The ceiling was twenty feet above the floor, which Mountjoy regarded as reasonable, for he was a man of extensive vision. As a boy he had loved to lie on the same couch when the bedroom was his father's and indulge his fantasies among the lions and unicorns and roses. He dreamed, then, of knights and maidens, and the glint of armor in a wintry sun and the ancient shout "à Mountjoy!

à Mountjoy" with which his forefathers had rallied the little army of Grand Fenwick around the banner of the double-headed eagle, when courage ebbed and men's hearts needed lifting up again.

Now, a grown man, indeed an almost venerable man, prime minister of the tiny Duchy of Grand Fenwick, tucked into a fold of the Alps between France and Switzerland, he had the same fancies. He regarded himself as the guardian and protector of Grand Fenwick, founded by the first duke, Roger Fenwick, in 1370, by the unanswerable logic of a broadsword and fifty English bowmen determined to carve a nation for themselves out of the welter of European dukedoms. Yes, the protector of the nation now six hundred years old, and all its traditions. More than that, the protector of the traditions of Europe itself and thus of all Western civilization.

He was certainly the oldest living statesman in Europe. He had served his gracious lady, Gloriana XII, for thirty years and her father for thirty before. He was, he supposed, eighty years of age, though this did not seem in the slightest degree possible. Still he could remember from his boyhood the Great War and later the Italian invasion of Abyssinia, the Spanish Civil War, the Second World War, the Korean War. (He had warned President Truman in a letter that confrontation was inevitable under the peace treaty which had disarmed Japan. In return he had received a photograph of the President, with, written at the bottom, the words "Like hell—Harry.") He'd seen the Vietnam War and the Laotian war and the Cambodian war and he regarded all these wars as the work of bunglers who had come to think of themselves as statesmen.

Reflectively examining the ceiling it occurred to him

12

that Derek of Pirenne had put more into his work than he, Mountjoy, had previously seen. He decided to look more closely into the man and his history. The design was obviously symbolic. The graceful white unicorns represented statesmen: educated, refined, intellectual minds attacked, but never destroyed, by the aggressive, unthinking lions. The entwining roses were the flowers and riches of civilization for which the two contested. Fanciful, perhaps, and yet there was something solid in the interpretation.

The Tompion clock which stood by a lancet window of the vast bedchamber struck three and Mountjoy pulled the bell cord which dangled beside his huge fourposter bed. Then he wandered into his study in the adjoining chamber and sat at his desk. The mail, which came by bus (nothing in the world would persuade the French postal authorities that diplomatic mail to Grand Fenwick should be sent by special conveyance) would be delivered at any moment.

It was collected at the border by Bill Treadwick, the postmaster, who then rode his bicycle with it to the castle, for delivery to Mountjoy.

Treadwick was getting a bit old, and the distance of something over two miles was mostly uphill. The journey took him about an hour and sometimes longer, for he was not above stopping at the Grey Goose, the only tavern in Grand Fenwick, for a pint of beer, or, on Saturdays, a glass of wine.

Once he had left an important cablegram for Mountjoy on the taproom bar and half the nation had known of its contents before it was finally delivered to the Prime Minister. The memory irked Mountjoy deeply, for it had been a key event in the chain of unlucky chance which had brought about the downfall of President Nixon.

The matter is worth a brief note to set the chronicle of those unhappy times straight. In the midst of the crisis, which Mountjoy had decided to ignore as part of the astonishing naïveté of Americans in political affairs, the hot water system in the castle had broken down. The system had been installed at American expense as an essential part of the peace treaty between the United States and Grand Fenwick bringing an end to the war between the two nations which Grand Fenwick had won, the details of which are recorded elsewhere.*

Before the installation of the American hot water system, the water for Mountjoy's bath had had to be heated in the kitchen several floors below and brought up in buckets, by which time it was no longer hot but tepid. The American water heater was, then, for Mountjoy, an important part of the treaty of peace. When the system broke down, Mountjoy immediately cabled Nixon, "Send plumbers."

The harassed President, thinking he was receiving advice concerning White House leaks, had gratefully cabled Mountjoy, "Thank you for your wise advice. Have started plumbing operations. Anticipate happiest results here. Pat sends her love. Ever yours. Dick." He had then launched that secret investigation into the affairs of Ellsberg and others which rebounded so horribly against him.

It was this cablegram which had lain on the taproom bar of the Grey Goose for several days before delivery to Mountjoy. By the time he received it and realized that the President had utterly mistaken his request as a piece of advice concerning his own domestic troubles, the

* See *The Mouse That Roared*.

14

damage was already done and the White House had begun to topple.

The daily mail delivery, then, was a time of anxiety for the Count of Mountjoy; a time when his patience was sorely tried and a time when he was often indignant that the affairs of the nation should be so frequently in the hands of an aging postman.

On this particular day the mail, when it arrived, contained little of note—a letter from a lady in Chicago who had lost a pair of shoes, size seven, while visiting the castle of Grand Fenwick, and was appealing to Mountjoy to find them for her, all other appeals having failed; a circular advertising the sale of three racehorses in Ireland and an airmail copy of the London *Times*, three days out of date thanks to the French, and a short handwritten note from Benjamin Rustin, Secretary of the Interior of the United States, which read:

Dear Al:
The full impact of the energy crisis is something we are going to have to face eventually, but in view of the political situation we are not playing it up until after the elections. You understand of course how the sins of previous administrations are always blamed on the incumbent and it is the consensus here that the only way to duck is to adopt a position of calm and confidence. But we have to have a plan eventually on which as you may imagine many experts in my department are working. We will not propose anything that might be hurtful in your many areas without first consulting you. In the meantime if there is anything you can do to make us look good as the crisis looms, we'll all be grateful.
Benjy.

The Count of Mountjoy read through this letter twice before concluding that he had been perhaps too hard on the postal service of France and the postal service of the United States was not, in the words of Katherine, his seven-year-old great-grandchild, winning any Brownie points. Then he examined the envelope and realized that the error had nothing to do with the postal service but was the fault of some clerk on the staff of the United States Minister for the Interior. The envelope was plainly addressed to him. In short, Al, whoever he was, had received a letter intended for the Duchy of Grand Fenwick, and he had received this missive with a hint at least of political chicanery intended for the mysterious Al.

This was worrying. The letter for him would obviously be on a matter of importance entrusted by the State Department which did not want to be found in direct correspondence with Grand Fenwick, to the Department of the Interior. So Mountjoy reasoned, for he had years of experience in the deviousness of intergovernmental correspondence. The note dealt with a sensitive matter, then, on which secrecy was essential. Now Al, whoever he was, knew all about it and he, Mountjoy, had only this piece of blather about the energy crisis in compensation.

"Damnation," he cried. "The world is full of blunderers and there is a rising tide of carelessness everywhere, the finest product of the modern system of education, which will sweep us all into the dark ages." He reached for the telephone to call Henry Thatcher, the U.S. Secretary of State, holding that he was certainly the person who should be told of this miscarriage of correspondence. Direct dialing not yet having reached Grand Fenwick, he gave the number to the Grand Fenwick operator, who gave it to the French operators, who gave it to the international operator. The message would be bounced off a communications satellite in some manner which Mountjoy could not understand and with which he disagreed in principle as belittling the function of the heavens.

After a brief silence he heard a ringing tone and then a voice came on the line that said, "I am sorry. The number you have called is no longer in service. Please consult your latest directory or ask your operator for assistance."

"Idiot!" cried Mountjoy. "I'm calling the United States of America. Are you going to tell me that it is no longer in service?" He hung up and tried again, but this time all the lines were busy. There were eight telephone lines in Grand Fenwick. Two lines were supposed to be reserved at all times for Mountjoy's use. But the operators were easygoing and democratic by nature. They thought it no sin to allow others to use the reserved lines when there was a flood of calls.

Mountjoy, after several futile attempts to get a free line, put the telephone down and stared at the wall. The world, he was aware, was full of incompetents—the result of cruelly attempting to educate the lower classes beyond their ability. There was an easygoing camaraderie among these allowing little or no respect for those in authority or of superior knowledge.

At that moment Meadows, his butler, appeared, answering the summons on the bell pull with a tray on which there gleamed a silver teapot in the Regency style, a silver milk jug, a silver sugar bowl with sugar tongs in the form of eagles' claws, and two Royal Doulton teacups and saucers.

Mountjoy glanced at the two teacups and then at Meadows, who put the tray down on a low table and said, "Her Grace has signified a desire to visit you for a cup of tea, sir."

Mountjoy was touched and at the same time a trifle mortified. It was gracious of his sovereign lady, Gloriana XII of Grand Fenwick, to leave her own chambers to have tea with him, gracious and in keeping with her character. But he was mortified by the thought that she had been coming to have tea with him more and more frequently in recent months, and this might be because she thought him a trifle old and not up to the task of walking up the two flights of stairs to visit her in her own quarters.

"Excellent," he said. "Orange pekoe, I trust."

"Yes, my lord," said Meadows, "but Her Grace has recently been drinking plain Lipton's—in a tea bag."

"Good God," cried Mountjoy. "Is she sick?"

"No, my lord," replied Meadows. "Quite well."

"That's the influence of Bentner," growled Mountjoy. "The fellow has been drinking plain Lipton's out of tea bags for years, and his mind has become increasingly sluggish as a result." David Bentner, a mere whippersnapper of sixty-four, was the founder of the Grand Fenwick Labor Party and leader, at the present time, of Her Grace's Loyal Opposition in the Parliament of Grand Fenwick—the Council of Freemen.

Her Grace entered alone. She was wearing an afternoon gown of some flowered material and looked to Mountjoy like a girl of perhaps seventeen—with a fresh loveliness which had never deserted her through the years. She was in fact in her mid-forties, though still acknowledged one of the ruling beauties of Europe.

"Your servant," said Mountjoy, rising to meet her.

"Bobo," replied Gloriana, "when you say that I still

18

get a little quiver. Did you see the movie about Disraeli and Victoria? Do you think he was really in love with her?"

"Service is love, Your Grace," said Mountjoy quietly, "and in that sense I am sure that Disraeli loved Victoria as much as I have loved Your Grace for thirty years."

"You're such a darling, Bobo," said Gloriana. "Remember, you used to take me for picnics when I was a child? I never told you before but when I was little and the wind was blowing and making a horrible noise around the Jerusalem Tower of the castle, near my bedroom, I used to imagine you standing guard at the end of my bed and it made me feel quite safe."

"You were a pretty child, Your Grace," said Mountjoy, "as you are now a beautiful woman." Another matter, the remarriage of the Duchess, who had been a widow now for ten years, presented itself, but he pushed the question aside. The mood was wrong and the timing too. He dismissed Meadows and with a thin and aristocratic hand reached for the teapot.

"I'll pour," Gloriana said. "Did you stir it?"

"No," Mountjoy replied. "It's Grey's orange pekoe. It should never be stirred since stirring releases a suspicion of tannin, which crushes the delicate flavor."

"Oh," said Gloriana. "Sorry. Lipton's isn't bad when you get used to it and it costs very much less."

"The money cost may be less," Mountjoy said. "The cost to so delicate a palate as yours is hardly to be borne. Pray, Your Grace, why do you touch such a mixture?"

"We have to economize," Gloriana said. "Bentner says so and I think he's right, you know. It's something to do with the energy shortage, which everybody seems to think is going to get worse. If you use Lipton's in a tea bag, you

19

need only one cup of boiling water and that saves on fuel. Bentner gave me some figures to show that if everyone switched to tea bags, instead of using loose orange pekoe or something grand in pots, the world saving in energy cost in ten years would amount to the total output of the sun for half a day. Something like that."

"And the death of millions from indigestion," said Mountjoy. "Bentner's a fool. You can, as I have often told Your Grace, recognize a fool by the fact that he always argues from statistics. Statistics, at best, may give us a rough picture of things as they are at the moment. But they are utterly unreliable as a basis for reasoning, for they make the unwarrantable assumption that the proportions and desires of the past will be the proportions and desires of the future. It is fallacious to assume that you can learn anything about humanity from statistics. Two lumps of sugar, if I may."

Gloriana dutifully put the two lumps of sugar in his cup and watched with how steady a hand he took it from her. Mountjoy had always distrusted statistics. There was a quality in the Count of Mountjoy which was at constant odds with the cold logic of calculators, a quality which made him champion of humanity with all its errors, against the rigid rules of science.

"Bobo," Gloriana said, "what is this energy talk all about? Is it something that is going to affect us here in Grand Fenwick?"

Mountjoy took a judicious sip of his tea, delighted that the subtle flavor of the orange pekoe found its perfect counterpart in the two lumps of sugar. He put his cup down with a steady hand and said, "It's a sort of international bogeyman which has been raising its head for the past fifteen years or more and has been ignored bv everyone as being politically and economically too hot to handle. It dates at least from the better days of President Nixon, who once rather foolishly assured the United States that America had no real need of oil from the Arabian countries and could get along quite well without it. That was a highly popular statement at the time though quite without foundation.

"The truth is that America, doing all it could for the state of Israel, and rightly too, happened at the time to have all its energy eggs in an Arabian basket. Now they have to look around for some different eggs or face mounting prices and a possible serious shortage of oil."

"It's serious then," Gloriana said. "All those people over there riding bicycles and jogging through the streets —is that part of it?"

"No," Mountjoy said, "that is part of the American dream of eternal youth. Americans will have nothing at all to do with the wisdom and serenity of age. But then, after all, they are a very young nation, scarcely two hundred years old."

"Well, Bentner thinks that it is going to affect everybody," said the Duchess. "He says it's going to produce an enormous rise in the cost of living and it may bring about a huge depression—'the collapse of society as we know it now' was the phrase he used."

"In my lifetime," said Mountjoy, "I've lived through four or five collapses of society and the only one that really bothered me was the disappearance of the horse. The automobile is not an adequate substitute.

"But Your Grace should not be concerned. I have the matter well before me and propose to get in touch with the United States on the subject. As Your Grace well knows, there have been several occasions in the past when we in Grand Fenwick have been able to put to rights matters which seemed beyond the competence of greater nations."

When she had left, Mountjoy remained for a long time thinking about Bentner, the energy crisis and the misdirected letter which lay on the table before him. The energy crisis was one he had been long aware was coming, though in the United States it was apparent that the political implications were more immediately worrying to the administration than the unavoidable economic impact.

Grand Fenwick, which scarcely used any oil energy at all, would hardly be affected. Still Grand Fenwick had a duty to the world and to its close ally, the United States of America. He must think of some plan for avoiding the crisis and present it at the proper moment. The enormity of the project cheered him immediately and he poured himself another cup of orange pekoe as a sort of celebration.

CHAPTER

2

The Al for whom the misdirected letter to the Count of Mountjoy had been intended was Alfonso Birelli, Chairman of the Board of Transcontinental Enterprises, a conglomerate whose holdings and interests included shipping, airlines, steel, railroads, real estate, electronics, three publishing houses, twenty television stations and Pentex Oil, a mammoth producing, refining, importing and distributing company; the largest in fact in the world.

Physically he was of a size to match his position—a tall gray wolf of a man, big-boned, with a lean face, cold as frost, though capable now and then of a glint of humor. He was fond of saying that he had come up the hard way, for his father had been a millionaire and his grandfather too.

"To be born wealthy is a crippling. handicap, which only the toughest survive," he said. "My whole life has been devoted to proving that I am not just the mentally impotent son of a rich man." He had proven it abundantly, over and over again, but those who thought of him as merely a financial and industrial wizard now completely misunderstood him. He was instead a warrior, a fighter, a lover of hazard and of battle; a man who would risk everything to gain his end; and the various companies over which he ruled were a testament to how well his daring had served him. They were for him the spoils of war in which he was always more daring than his enemies.

His name, even his existence, was quite unknown to the American public at large. Indeed there were many newsmen in the higher strata of press, television and radio who had never heard of him.

Those at the very top were aware of Alfonso Birelli merely as a Power.

It was rumored that he had close connections with the Mafia and it was also said that he had close connections with the White House, but this in a sense belittled him.

It would be more true to say that the Mafia and the White House even had some close connections with Alfonso Birelli, for he had enough muscle to do favors, when he wished, for both. Nor did it matter to him who at any particular time occupied the White House or was the nation's chief Godfather. Whoever they might be, there would come a time when they would need support from Alfonso Birelli.

It was in keeping with his lone-wolf character that he occupied no luxurious suite of offices but conducted his business from two rooms, furnished in the fashion of the nineteen-thirties, on the twentieth floor of a venerable building on Wall Street.

There were a desk, a swivel chair, a few filing cabinets

and a secretary, Miss Thompson, a woman in her late fifties—plump, sweet and motherly, and hard as a stainless steel nail. She handled all his telephone calls, all his mail and all his appointments. She alone knew where he was at all times and she alone knew who might speak to him and who might not.

Miss Thompson was surprised, then, one morning, in opening his mail, to find a letter from the Secretary of the Interior, announcing a meeting of American vintners and inviting him to send a representative.

She glanced quickly at the top of the letter, found that it was addressed to the Count of Mountjoy, Duchy of Grand Fenwick, and threw it in the wastepaper basket.

Then she reflected that there actually was a Duchy of Grand Fenwick and that the Duchy of Grand Fenwick had on several occasions in the past made a not inconsiderable mark on the United States of America and world history.

She glanced at the envelope, which was addressed to Alfonso Birelli, and realized that a mistake had been made.

Any mistake which involved her employer might have, she knew, serious consequences, so she retrieved the letter from the wastepaper basket, put it with the half dozen other communications she had decided should be brought to his attention and glanced at the electric coffeepot on a shelf beside her small desk.

It was perking briskly. Alfonso Birelli liked a mug of piping-hot coffee brought in with his mail. She poured out the coffee, put the mug on a tray with the letters and took them in to him, first giving the connecting door a gentle kick with her foot, which was her way of announcing her presence.

"Morning," said Birelli without glancing up. "Cancel that seat on the Concorde to Paris. Tell Hastings that I'm not going and buy a thousand shares of Etienne et Cie. They'll be down a point and a half when word gets around. What have you got that's funny?"

"Funny" was his word for important, and she gave him the selected mail, with the Grand Fenwick letter on the bottom. He glanced through the letters and without the slightest exchange of expression read the Grand Fenwick communication to which the envelope was pinned.

"Son of a bitch," he said thoughtfully, looking from the envelope to the letter. "This means that the Count of Mountjoy has got hold of some communication intended for me. The last person in the world I want knowing anything about my business is Mountjoy. That guy's either the smartest statesman since Machiavelli or the biggest fool ever to hold public office. I've never been able to decide which."

"It's from the Department of the Interior," said Miss Thompson somewhat unnecessarily. "Shall I call the Secretary, explain the situation, and ask him what his letter was about?"

"Get him on the phone," said Birelli grimly. "I'll speak to him myself."

When the call was put through he picked up the phone and said "Benjy? Al here. You know something? I don't give a hang about attending a meeting of the nation's wine growers. Now what else did you have in mind?"

With such an introduction it took a little while before the Secretary of the Interior grasped the situation, apologized for the error and said his note had contained a reference to the energy crisis, to the low profile the government was going to assume on the matter, to the fact that many were working on plans to soften or avert the crisis when the full extent of the oil shortage became known to the public, that nothing would be done without his first being consulted, and concluded with a request that he lend whatever help he could to the administration when the time arrived.

"As far as covering up," snapped Birelli on hearing this, "you're about four innings behind in the ball game right now. Mountjoy knows the contents of that letter and he's probably leaked it to half a dozen chancelleries right at this moment."

"I hardly think so," said the Secretary. "He's not what I would call a prime source of news of international importance among the governments of Europe."

"Listen," said Birelli. "Anything to do with oil, oil prices, oil shortages—anything at all—including U.S. government concern about oil—hurts me where I'm very sensitive. Right now I don't want the full facts about the energy crisis to become public any more than the President does. In fact, I can't think of a time when I would be willing to let the facts be known to the public. I've already outlined four plans of my own for dealing with the situation when it arises, but now I have to take into consideration that Mountjoy has been alerted to the coming crisis. Maybe it will mean nothing to him." He paused while he thought of all he knew of Mountjoy and Grand Fenwick. "Maybe it might even be helpful," he said softly, as Plan Number Five began to take shape in his active mind.

"What might be helpful?" asked the Secretary of the Interior.

"Never mind," said Birelli. "Just bear this in mind. I'm going to be able to handle the crisis myself without any of your boys from the nation's law schools screwing things up, provided nobody announces that there is a crisis. A crisis is only a crisis when somebody in authority calls it a crisis. Get that around to the presidential staff, too, will you? If they don't understand it, tell them to start reading a book called *The Prince* by Machiavelli. We've avoided three depressions in the last twenty years by calling them recessions and we can do the same with this oil shortage provided nobody blows the whistle.

"Anyway, leave it to me. I'll handle it and Mountjoy as well. Just stick to the low-profile idea and hire somebody over there who has brains enough to put the right letters in the right envelopes."

With that he hung up and took a huge sip of his coffee, no longer boiling hot, his mind busy with Mountjoy, the Duchy of Grand Fenwick and the oil crisis. He canceled all his appointments for the day, told Miss Thompson not to put any phone calls through to him, and by three o'clock in the afternoon he put through a telephone call to France. When the call was concluded and Miss Thompson, in answer to his summons, entered his office to take some dictation, she noted a glint of a smile in his eyes, and knew that he had launched a plan which pleased him well and would have a tremendous impact upon the world.

The Duchy of Grand Fenwick's oil consumption was the lowest in the whole of Europe, for the tiny nation had no factories, no railroads, no buses, no airplanes, a very small power station and but two automobiles—a Daimler belonging to Her Grace which she used for occasional shopping trips in France or Switzerland, and a Rolls-Royce which Mountjoy had inherited from his father. The Daimler dated from 1947 and the Rolls, a superb Silver Ghost, from 1927. Whenever Gloriana wanted to move about in Grand Fenwick, she walked or rode her bicycle, and Mountjoy walked also, though recently finding himself a trifle stiff, he was sometimes chauffeured around in the Rolls.

Some days after receiving the letter intended for Birelli, Mountjoy decided to go for a drive in the Rolls both to get some air and to call on Bentner, who lived in a small cottage close to the French frontier three miles from the castle.

Bentner, though he had made a considerable fortune from his sheep and his vineyards which together with the others of the Duchy produced that noble wine, Pinot Grand Fenwick, insisted on living in this humble dwelling, which was lit by oil lamps and where all the cooking was done on a woodburning range. This was in keeping with his position as founder of the Grand Fenwick Labor Party.

He took a weekly bath in a huge tin tub with water heated on the same range, and he always took the bath in the kitchen, ordering everybody out. Then, with the fire glowing and the water deliciously heated, he stepped into his vast tin tub—pink, fat and a trifle wrinkled—and luxuriated for forty minutes or more. Sometimes he fell asleep in the tub, and Mrs. Marsden, his housekeeper, falling to wake him by hammering on the door, would have to come in and rouse him, naked and rosy, fat and content.

When this had happened half a dozen times, Bentner married her as being the decent thing to do in the circumstances. After their marriage he still called her Mrs.

Marsden and she still called him Mr. Bentner. They had borne those names too long to change. But they had a sort of pudding love for each other—quiet and comfortable and based on deep mutual respect.

Mountjoy thought Bentner a fool, though he was fond of him. "He has the brain of a somnolent oyster," he once said, but he knew that there was in Bentner and his followers in the Labor Party a kind of plodding sense essential to the political structure of Grand Fenwick.

Mountjoy was not an autocrat. He was a democrat in that true sense of the word which permits the aristocracy and the commonalty to staunchly champion their own viewpoints without despising each other. The Church, of course, stood patiently neutral, properly calling upon God to bless both sides. "A tolerance of which only God is capable," as Abbot Ambrose, of the tiny monastery lodged in the equally tiny forest of Grand Fenwick, pointed out.

There was but one gasoline pump in Grand Fenwick to serve the two automobiles of the Duchy. It was operated by Bert Green, who ran the bicycle shop in the village and added to his living by grazing twenty plump sheep on a mountainside pasture. He sold a few new bicycles, mostly around Christmas, and all of them of English manufacture—Raleighs, BSAs and Rudge-Whitworths for the most part.

Mountjoy then called for his Rolls and, putting on his motoring cap and greatcoat and gloves, descended to the courtyard. He told the chauffeur to drive him to Bentner's place and the chauffeur, touching his cap, said he would have to stop in the village for petrol. He coasted the car down through the village street to Bert Green's bicycle shop and stopped before the old-fashioned, hand-operated gasoline pump.

"Fill her up," the chauffeur said to Bert and Bert looked at the pump and at the Rolls, took a stub of cigarette out of the corner of his mouth and crushed it slowly on the ground.

"Can't," he said. "There's only five gallons in the bottom of the sump. A lot of that's water and the pump can't reach it."

"What happened?" asked the chauffeur. "Sump leaking?"

"Nope," said Bert. "Bloomin' Frogs have cut us down to twenty gallons a month, and I put fifteen in Her Grace's Daimler day before yesterday. No more coming for a fortnight."

"And pray," said Mountjoy, who had overheard the exchange, "why are we to have only twenty gallons of petrol a month in Grand Fenwick?"

Bert shrugged. "Search me," he said. He went into the bicycle shop, rummaged in a drawer near the cash register where he kept bills, receipts, pencil stubs and a few tools, and came out with a grubby piece of paper. "Chap who came with the delivery truck gave me this. It's in French so I didn't read it." He handed Mountjoy a sheet of green paper with some italic printing on it, and some blank spaces filled in by hand in purple ink. Mountjoy glanced at the sheet. It was headed:

COMPAGNIE INTERNATIONALE DES PRODUITS
MAZOUT FRANCAIS

The text read:

> *Nous sommes obligés de vous aviser qu'à cause de la situation internationale regardant la provision des produits mazout, il est nécessaire de limiter sévèrement la distribution de l'essence. En conséquence*

une quote-part a été instituée et le lotissement de Bert Green à Grande Fenwick a été fixé à quatre-vingt litres chaque mois.

Charles Dupleixes
Président C.I.P.M.F.

The signature was rubber-stamped.

"When did you get this?" demanded Mountjoy.

"Last delivery—couple of weeks ago."

Mountjoy swallowed hard and was for the moment speechless. It was an outrage that he, the Prime Minister of a sovereign and independent nation, should be informed by a gasoline-station attendant that the supply of gasoline to his country was to be almost entirely cut off.

The thing was beyond bearing, and it cut deeper that he received the news on a printed form letter with a rubber-stamp signature. He would instantly send a telegram to the President of the French Republic couched in such terms as to have this fellow Dupleixes imprisoned in whatever the French now used as a substitute for the Bastille.

Meanwhile the chauffeur and Bert stood looking at him patiently and a horrible thought occurred to the Count.

"What about the fuel oil for heating my bath?" he asked. It came from the same supplier.

"Sent the last ten gallons up to the castle yesterday," said Bert. "Should last a week. Looks like we're not going to get any more."

"Damnation," cried Mountjoy. "The government of the United States of America is obliged, under a treaty approved by their own Senate, to supply me with hot water in perpetuum. This is an outrage. I shall not stand for it."

He had dismounted to inspect the letter Bert had pro-

duced and he now got back into the Rolls and slammed
the door.

"Drive on," he said to the chauffeur.

"Can't," the chauffeur replied. "We're out of gas."

CHAPTER

3

Grand Fenwick, then, became the first country in the world to feel at one blow the full effect of the energy shortage with Mountjoy reduced again to one bath a week, his bath water having to be heated on the woodburning kitchen stove below and brought up several flights of stairs as in previous years.

The twenty gallons of gasoline permitted under the French quota allowed the Duchess in her Daimler and Mountjoy in his Rolls to drive between them a total of eighty miles per month.

Mountjoy, true to his word, immediately sent off a strong letter of protest to the President of the French Republic and to the President of the United States.

From the first he received no reply.

From the second he received, after some while, a short note signed by Kurt Hannigan, Executive Assistant to the

President, assuring him that every effort was being made to increase oil production in the United States but adding that the situation in the Near East, coupled with the vastly expanding use of oil for fuel, made any immediate hope of relief improbable.

This was followed by a pamphlet from the Department of the Interior on how to insulate a house in order to cut down heating costs, emphasizing that the expenditure involved was deductible from income tax.

"Damn fools," exclaimed Mountjoy when he received the latter. "How do they expect me to insulate a castle? And what effect would stuffing the roof with some kind of artificial sponge rubber have on the temperature of my bath water? They've been bungling for years and we in Grand Fenwick are the first victims of their inspired incompetence. I insist that the terms of our peace treaty with the United States be carried out to the letter. I insist on my hot bath. I shall write again."

"I don't think it's the United States," said Bentner, to whom Mountjoy had been fulminating. "The Americans are nice people. Just a bit too trusting. It's them Arabs. They're the ones holding up the oil supply, creating a shortage and hoping for a rise in price. Supposing we were to send twenty longbowmen over there like when we invaded New York and capture a couple of oil wells for ourselves. Maybe even a refinery."

"Good Lord, Bentner," Mountjoy exclaimed. "Do you think we are back in the time of the Crusades with the Arabs riding around on camels dressed in flowing robes and armed with small shields and lances? Don't you realize that the Arab nations at the present time probably have an air force and armament of modern weapons, including rockets, sufficient to challenge Great Britain?"

Bentner considered this for a while and shook his head. "Where did they get them?" he asked.

"From the United States, of course. Great Britain and France as well, I suspect. They got a lot of money for their oil. Billions of pounds and bought arms in return. Largely because of the Israel situation. As I see it, we in Grand Fenwick are caught in a conflict between Moses and Mohammed with the result that I cannot get a hot bath.

"You don't suppose they'd have any use for a score of longbows and a few bushels of arrows?" asked Bentner.

"No. I certainly don't. We'll have to think of something else. First I am going to insist that the terms of our peace treaty with the United States are implemented to the letter. Then I see that I'm going to have to put my mind to the solving of the oil problem on a worldwide scale. Civilization cannot exist and progress without a plentiful and cheap supply of fuel oil. But if this is truly a shortage and not a piece of manipulation to drive oil prices up, an alternative source of energy is plainly called for. I'll talk to Dr. Kokintz about it. After all, the man who developed the Q, or quadium, bomb singlehanded should readily be able to come up with an inexpensive method of heating water and running an automobile."

The prospect roused him. He, Mountjoy, was once again going to take a hand in saving the world from its follies.

"Bentner," he said. "We are going to have to stand shoulder to shoulder in this crisis. The question is not one of politics but of the salvation of society. What has happened here now in Grand Fenwick will shortly be happening all over the world. People will be shivering in their homes, their automobiles motionless in their garages, their great factories closing down one by one, and with each closing, thousands put out of work and unable to use their Visa cards. That in itself will put thousands more out of work, shake the financial foundation of many great corporations, and spread gloom and despair like a plague through the domain of Western Man. Western civilization stands at its greatest crisis—a crisis involving not freedom of speech nor of thought nor of worship, but the equally great freedom to live at some level of dignity and comfort above that of a medieval peasant. Something must be done. You and I must do it."

"Look," said Bentner, "aren't you making a bit too much fuss about not getting a hot bath? Do what I do. Put the tub down in front of the fireplace in the kitchen, kick everybody out and enjoy yourself. Let the world solve its own problems. We've got enough wood here to last us for centuries."

"Bah," Mountjoy said. "I will not be driven back to the sixteenth century by half a million Arabs who seem to have made a captive of every brain in America. Forward, I say, into the thick of the battle, and let the banner of Grand Fenwick lead the way."

"Still think you ought to try having a bath in front of the kitchen fire first," said Bentner.

The interview had taken place in Mountjoy's study in the castle. When it was over Mountjoy decided to call immediately on Dr. Kokintz, who, as noted, was the inventor of the appalling Q-bomb which Grand Fenwick had captured during its war against the United States.

Kokintz, now a citizen of Grand Fenwick, had his office and laboratory in the dungeon of the main keep of the castle, and there he carried out various experiments of which Mountjoy knew little and cared less.

Kokintz was dressed as usual in a rumpled pullover, a pair of shoddy trousers and a jacket of his own design. It was without a collar or lapels but had numerous pockets in which Kokintz kept pencils and pens and scraps of paper on which he made cabalistic calculations. In the side pockets he kept crackers and pieces of bread with which to feed the birds during his daily walks about Grand Fenwick, for he was very fond of birds and prided himself more as an ornithologist than as a physicist.

When Mountjoy entered, Kokintz was seated at a long table, littered with retorts, Bunsen burners, spirals of glass tubing which connected with series of bottles, an apparatus for producing old-fashioned ruby laser rays and another, not yet completed and of his own design, a white laser capable of penetrating a foot of high-tensile steel. All around were cages of birds: some pets and others he was treating for a sickness or injury. He was at the moment tying a lump of something white to a long piece of string.

"What's that?" Mountjoy asked.

"Suet," Kokintz said. "I hang it in the garden. It helps the birds get enough fat when seeds and berries are getting scarce."

When he had finished tying the piece of suet to the string he held it up smiling with pleasure.

"The titmice will love it," he said.

"I suppose they will," said Mountjoy, who didn't give a hang for titmice. "Actually I came to talk to you about the energy crisis and perhaps get you working on the problem. Do you have any thoughts on energy?" The question was as close as Mountjoy could come to being scientific.

"Energy," said Kokintz, vaguely, as if he had heard the

word somewhere. His mind was still on the suet. He took off his glasses and polished them on the hem of his pullover. "Energy," he repeated, putting his glasses back on his nose and pulling his mind together. "We are surrounded by energy. Everything we see or touch is energy in one form or another. Energy is something we will never run out of."

"Well, we just ran out of it," said the Count. "My Rolls is down in the village at this moment and utterly useless. We are out of petrol. Also heating oil."

Kokintz shrugged. "Oil is but one source of energy," he said. "A minor source, in fact, though the one that comes easiest to hand. But you are surely aware of solar energy in all its forms—radiation from the sun, winds, tides, the growth of vegetable matter and even ourselves. Yes, my friend, we are a result of solar energy, without which we would die.

"Then there is the energy to be obtained from coal, itself solar energy stored from the sunshine of billions of years ago, and from wood and from the burning or distillation of vegetable matter, and then of course there is nuclear energy, and the energy which results from the mysterious force known as gravity, though that source is perhaps but two percent of the energy available on earth. I might add the energy whose primary source is sound— a great deal of which is of course inaudible to the human ear, though we have instruments which can pick up much, but not all of it. We are, as you perhaps know, being constantly bombarded by energy from outer space, some of which consists of sounds and some of which can be transformed into sounds—"

"What about oil?" said Mountjoy, interrupting, for he knew from experience that once Kokintz started talking on any subject of scientific interest, he was all but unstoppable.

Kokintz puffed through his lips, which was a mannerism of his when he had been asked a question on a hopeless topic. He considered the vast swarm of the galaxies with their trillions of planets spinning around their billions of suns. He considered the possibility of organic life decomposing on these planets and turning into oil, oil shale and coal.

"There must be enough oil in outer space to drown the earth under a sea of it thousands of fathoms deep," he said.

"Never mind outer space," said the Count of Mountjoy testily. "I mean how about oil right here in Grand Fenwick, enough to run two motorcars and heat my bath, to start with."

Kokintz shook his head. "Most unlikely," he said. "The mountains are igneous rock—granite for the greater part. No oil-bearing formations. It would appear that Grand Fenwick was never subjected to the pressures and marine conditions which produce oil."

Mountjoy decided to try another tack.

"What are you working on right now?" he asked, looking over the complicated apparatus set up on the long table.

Kokintz, forgetting for the moment the laser on which he had been engaged for some months, said, "I'm making a kite for your great-granddaughter Katherine. A blue one," he added.

Mountjoy took a deep breath. His great-granddaughter, he well knew, was a persistent little being and had been bothering everybody she knew in the Duchy to make her a blue kite. Kokintz, one of the most eminent physicists in the Western world, had now been cornered into doing the job.

"Well," said Mountjoy, a trifle huffily, "when you get through with Katherine's kite, would you be good enough to turn your mind to the problem of finding a cheap and abundant source of energy other than oil, so that not only can I get a decent bath each day, but the whole of Western civilization can be saved from complete chaos." He then went back to his study to take up the matter again, this time quite firmly, with the President of the United States. Kokintz watched him go, shook his head and went out into the garden to hang up the piece of suet for the tit-mice. When he came back his mind was involved not with energy or lasers but with the design of a kite which could be readily flown by a seven-year-old child. For Kokintz, such problems were not unimportant.

CHAPTER

4

President John Miller of the United States was surrounded by worries, predominant among which was how long he was going to remain the President of the United States. Presidential elections, he well knew, swung not on the real needs and problems of the country, the greater part of which were quite unknown to the electorate, and if known would probably put them in a panic.

The presidential election at the moment swung on the issues of how warm it was going to be in people's houses in the coming winter, for the energy shortage was becoming more apparent (despite efforts to play it down) week by week, and how much gasoline they could look for to run their automobiles, and how many hostages foreign students were going to seize in American embassies.

The word had gone around that Americans were big oil users and therefore were wicked. Sometimes it wasn't just oil that the Americans were accused of using in Gargantuan quantities. It was energy. They used, it was said, with pious scorn, more energy than any other people on earth and the fact that they did more with the energy they used than any other people on earth was quite beside the point. Americans had become ogres, vampires, destroyers rather than leaders of mankind, and in their humanity they destroyed bluebirds, anchovies, pine trees, grass, grizzly bears, black people, the soul, the oceans of the world, and having left their footprints on the moon were probably intent upon doing the same thing there and through the whole of outer space if they were not stopped.

The old slogan "Yankee go home" had been replaced by "Yankee get lost," which was much more hurtful.

"If only they'd read our Constitution," the President said to Secretary of State Henry Thatcher, who was the first to arrive for an unscheduled cabinet meeting.

"If only we would read it ourselves," said the Secretary of State.

Present at the meeting, hurriedly summoned from various parts of Washington and indeed the United States, were the Secretaries of the Interior, Defense, Energy, Agriculture, State, Space and Electronics. The meeting had been called to discuss the three Es—Energy, Economy and Election. But it was the matter of Energy which dominated the meeting, for the other two depended upon it

The Secretary of Agriculture, Wayne Ritchers, a tall, red-faced man with a protruding underlip which gave him a perpetual pout, was asked what progress was being made in the production of alcohol from agricultural waste—a project which had been headlined about the country the last time the OPEC nations had announced an increase in the price of oil per barrel.

"Mr. President," he said, "by next year we hope to produce fifty million gallons of alcohol from this source. That represents an all-out effort as the program is set up now—that is to say, utilizing what is called agricultural waste by converting it into alcohol. But I'd like to point out, Mr. President, that there really isn't such a thing as agricultural waste except in the newspapers. It's all organic matter which can be plowed back into the soil in one form or another to bring along next year's crop—whatever that crop may be. It contains a large proportion of the phosphates and nitrates taken out of the soil to nourish the particular plant.

"Some of it is used for cattle, sheep and hog feed. Turn it all into alcohol and you'll have a rise in meat prices and a rise perhaps in the price of artificial fertilizers."

"Aren't you forgetting that there are hundreds of millions of acres of land—scrub land, desert land—which could be brought under cultivation to produce crops purely for conversion into alcohol?" asked the Secretary of Energy.

"Nope," said the Secretary of Agriculture. "And I'm not forgetting that from the point of view of the ecologists these lands—mostly federal lands, mind you—are the last disappearing traces of wilderness America. Most of them are national parks, state parks or parks of some kind. Millions of acres are leased for grazing.

"Start plowing them up for fuel for automobiles or for industry and you've really got a cat fight on your hands. You know what would be the effect of that kind of program on election prospects.

"One other point. Even if you can fight down the ecologists and the cattle people, I'd hate to think of the

44

effect on world opinion when the stories got around that we were growing food crops to run automobiles while millions were starving in Africa, Cambodia and elsewhere. I think we'd lose a lot more embassies."

The President wasn't amused. "What you're telling me," he said, "is that only a very small percentage of our energy problems can be solved by the decomposition of farm wastes."

"That's right," said the Secretary of Agriculture. "Ignoring the actual supply, turning grain or any vegetable matter into alcohol is an expensive business, as I'm sure you found out the last time you bought a fifth of bourbon."

"A lot of that was tax," said the Secretary of the Treasury.

"So's a lot of the price of gasoline and fuel oil," replied the Secretary of Agriculture. "And you can't even drink the stuff."

There was more discussion on the subject, mostly wearying and negative, before the Secretary of the Interior, Benjamin Rustin, whose misdirected note on the energy crisis had wound up in the hands of the Count of Mountjoy, went over the coal situation in a few brief sentences which were only a restatement of what they all knew. There were enough coal reserves, both bituminous and anthracite, in the continental United States to supply the nation's energy needs for two hundred years, allowing for a vast increase in the demand for power over that time.

But it wouldn't be cheap power. The cost of extracting coal, of storing it, of transporting and distributing it was rising fast and would continue to rise.

"It was that cost, plus the pollution factor, you will recall, Mr. President, that brought about our greater

45

and greater dependence on oil," Rustin said. "Railroads switched to diesel and so did shipping, including the Navy.

"If we switch back again and on the increased basis now demanded, we'll have a pollution problem far beyond anything we've ever known. Hundreds of thousands of factory chimneys pouring pollutants into the air, and I'm not just talking about smoke. I'm talking about ammonia and sulfur and carbon monoxide gas and so on. Sure we can have controls and sure we can strive to develop ways of extracting these pollutants before they reach the atmosphere. But they will take a lot of time to develop and a lot of money to enforce.

"Coal isn't an immediate solution even as far as household heating is concerned. Also it's about the most wasteful solution we can come up with."

"Wasteful?" said the President.

"Yes, sir. There are something like two hundred thousand by-products which can be extracted from coal, many of which are going to be desperately needed in the future and the majority of which are utterly lost when coal is burned. What we need right now in my view—what we have to have, not only to solve the mounting energy crisis but to put a brake on world inflation, is a cheap and abundant and instantly available source of energy. Coal is not the solution."

So the talks went on. Solar energy was discussed in some detail, but while all agreed it was a tremendous potential power source, they also agreed that the cost of conversion was enormous and the technical problems of storing solar energy formidable.

It was decided that the President would announce an intensive research program into a cheap method of mass-producing solar cells to heat the homes of America. The announcement at least would cost nothing and might reap a harvest of needed votes. Nuclear energy was scarcely mentioned. It had become, following the Three Mile Island incident, the Boston Massacre of nuclear physics.

The conference ended with nothing new proposed and on a note of pessimism. When they had all left the President reflected gloomily that he had lived to see the day when the United States was spending millions of dollars on the erection of windmills as a source of power, putting the nation on a level with the Dutch in the sixteenth century. The consensus of the meeting had been that the country should go back to burning coal and handle the pollution problem as it arose.

"Backward," the President said to himself. "We're going backward. We're exploring the satellites of Jupiter and looking to power sources four and five hundred years old. This nation has lost more than sources of fuel. It's lost its self-confidence and imagination. We go around apologizing for everything we do. A hundred years ago we were laying down railroads from coast to coast and fighting the hell out of the Indians. Now we're apologizing for laying down the railroads and the Indians are fighting the hell out of us.

"Unless we get a grip on ourselves we're lost. Our greatest national output will be abject apologies to anyone who says we've trodden on their toes."

He picked up an advance copy of *Time* magazine and leafed through it nervously, and his eye fell on an advertisement for Franklin woodburning stoves. He dropped the magazine into the wastepaper basket and somehow felt a lot better.

CHAPTER

5

Mountjoy's second letter to the President of the United States was a simple one and in view of the Count's irritation it was almost good-natured. It read:

"Dear Mr. President:

"As you are aware, there is in existence a treaty of peace and mutual aid between the United States of America and the Duchy of Grand Fenwick containing various general provisions under which each country will help the other in time of need, if called upon, and specific provisions aimed at perpetuating the peace between your nation and mine.

"One specific provision of this treaty has unfortunately been broken without, I am sure, your knowledge or that of the Senate of the United States. I refer to Article XXXII, paragraph 12, subparagraph 3a, which reads, 'The Government of the United States further undertakes to ensure that there shall at all times be an efficient method of heating the castle of Grand Fenwick and of supplying the occupants of said castle with an ample amount of hot running water.

" 'If the United States should fail in this regard, then the matter shall be drawn directly to the attention of the President of the United States, who will issue the instructions needed to remedy the situation.'

"I respectfully wish, Mr. President, to call your attention to the fact that four weeks ago I addressed a letter to you on this subject but received in reply a communication from your Mr. Hannigan referring to various tensions in the Near East (of which this government is quite aware) and a pamphlet issued by your Department of the Interior on methods of insulating houses to reduce fuel costs.

"I cannot, even with the greatest goodwill, regard this as a sufficient fulfillment of the obligations of the United States under the article already referred to. I must therefore ask that instructions be issued for the immediate and continuous supply of sufficient fuel oil to carry out the provisions of this particular article.

"May I, at the same time, Mr. President, assure you that I have the fullest sympathy with your administration in the crisis which must arise when the full impact of the energy shortage becomes known to the public. In this respect, a mild winter in your northern States would be of the greatest benefit. I am aware that it is not uncommon for governments to be rudely shaken by the weather.

"The picture, however, is larger than any one nation, and with this in mind I have instructed Dr. Kokintz to concentrate his research on the whole problem of energy and, with the agreement of my own advisers, have set aside a substantial sum to be devoted to this research."

The substantial sum to which the Count of Mountjoy referred was an amount of two hundred Grand Fenwick pounds, totaling a little over four hundred dollars in American currency. Even for Grand Fenwick that could hardly be called a substantial sum, but Mountjoy excused the term on the grounds of diplomatic need. He had in mind applying for a loan at a later date to forward the research as soon as Kokintz reported any kind of progress.

As with the previous correspondence, this letter was fielded by Hannigan, who sent it over to the Central European Desk of the State Department with the notation "Please advise." Peter Wormsley, who was the official in charge of that section of the State Department, puzzled over the letter for half an hour trying to decide on its real meaning. That the real meaning was plainly set out in the letter itself did not occur to him at all, for his many years in the State Department had taught him that this was rarely the case. The phrase "the crisis which must arise when the full impact of the energy shortage becomes known to the public" bothered him, followed as it was by the reference to the atomic physicist Kokintz. The only crisis he could think of was the embarrassment of the President in seeking reelection in November with the greater part of the nation shivering in their homes and lining up for gasoline at service stations. But that was too obvious and therefore could not possibly be the crisis to which the Count of Mountjoy was referring.

He picked up the telephone and pressed a series of buttons which played a tune which sounded remarkably like "Oh Dear, What Can the Matter Be?" He wondered, not for the first time, who the joker was who had arranged that combination of numbers for Central Filing.

"Johnson here," said a voice at the other end.

"Wormsley, Central Europe. Please send me the situation file on Grand Fenwick."

"Grand who?"

"Grand Fenwick. The Duchy of Grand Fenwick."

There was a slight pause while Johnson considered whether someone was pulling his leg. He was new in the department, an earnest and humorless young man who had once spent two hours looking for the file on the Electorate of Brandenburg before discovering (in the Britannica) that the Electorate had been merged into the Kingdom of Prussia in 1701.

"The Duchy of Grand Fenwick," he said at length. "Okay. It may take a little time. They've misplaced Saudi Arabia. It's somewhere between here and the White House."

"Hang Saudi Arabia," said Wormsley. "I want that file on my desk in five minutes." He hung up and pressed some more buttons, being rewarded with a slightly off-key rendition of "My Bonnie Lies over the Ocean."

"Schilotz," he said. "Wormsley speaking. Would you be kind enough to drop by Central Filing, pick up the situation file on Grand Fenwick and bring it to me. We've got a problem."

"Okay," said Schilotz. He put the phone down and stared at it meditatively for a while. He was a fattish man who although in his mid fifties retained a look of boyishness, perhaps because his thinning hair was still blond and silken and his face and hands plump and unwrinkled.

His clothes had a boyish look, the jacket a little too tight and the pants uncreased and always slightly rumpled. He liked neutral colors and exuded a general air of timidity. He was an Aries and never failed to read his horoscope in the daily paper before reporting for work. His forecast for the day had read, "Pay attention to details. Small events may prove of the greatest importance. Be imaginative. Express yourself."

" 'Be imaginative. Express yourself,' " he repeated, went to Central Filing, picked up the Grand Fenwick folder and took it to Wormsley's office.

"What do you think of that?" Wormsley asked, throwing him Mountjoy's letter as soon as he was seated. Schilotz read it through, passed a plump hand over his fair, boyish hair and said, "Sounds serious." It was a safe thing to say because he knew that Wormsley never asked him to his office unless he was worried about something.

"What I don't like about it is that phrase about the crisis that must arise when the full impact of the energy shortage is known to the public, followed by the reference to Kokintz," Wormsley said. "What crisis? You don't suppose that that idiot Mountjoy is referring to the Q-bomb, do you?"

" 'Impact,' " Schilotz said. "That isn't the kind of word Mountjoy uses often. I'm pretty familiar with his style and I'd expect him to say 'effect' or 'outcome' or 'result'— something smooth. Impact is—explosive."

"Yes," Wormsley said, "and so's that damned Q-bomb. You know of course that Kokintz is the man who put that piece of damnation together. He was the first to identify and then produce quadium, a form of hydrogen which has not existed in the known universe for billions of years. The mass difference of the nucleus is greater than any other known element. That means that, size for size, it's more effective than anything else. But surely he's not threatening us. I mean Grand Fenwick threatening the United States?"

"Oh no," said Schilotz. "That would be over-reacting outrageously."

"Well, they went to war with us over a bottle of wine," Wormsley said. "They might do the same thing over a tub of hot water."

"Be imaginative," Schilotz said to himself, recalling his horoscope. Still, the concept of Grand Fenwick threatening the United States was surely being overimaginative. And yet in his letter Mountjoy made abundant and detailed reference to the terms of the treaty of peace between the United States and Grand Fenwick.

"There's the Strategic Arms Limitation Talks," he said tentatively. "Grand Fenwick is custodian of the Q-bomb and as far as we know they haven't revealed its composition, if that is the correct word, to anyone.

"If the treaty is broken, there's nothing to stop them from sharing it with the Russians. I don't say they would do that. Their whole sympathy lies with the United States. But the possibility exists—a remote possibility, but it is still there.

"In any case all that needs to be done, surely, is restore their supply of heating oil and gasoline. It doesn't amount to much. I can't understand why it was cut off or reduced in the first instance."

"Some bureaucratic foul-up," said Wormsley. "What are the details of supply, anyway?" Schilotz skimmed through the papers in the file and produced several slips of blue paper. "It seems that the Compagnie Internationale des Produits Mazout Français delivers the heating oil and gas to Grand Fenwick. Grand Fenwick pays the bill and then sends it, receipted, to us. They are reimbursed by the General Accounting Office. The French company, by the way, is a subsidiary of Pentex Oil."

"Pentex Oil," said Wormsley. "Pentex Oil." Something stirred in his memory, something about Pentex Oil he had overheard or been told at one of Washington's innumerable cocktail parties. He reached for the telephone, pressed a series of buttons ("Two Lovely Black Eyes"), reached the Commerce Department, asked for their Corporation Holding Section, identified himself and said, "Pentex Oil. I think they're part of a conglomerate. Can you check for me, please?"

"One moment."

Several minutes elapsed before the voice came back on the line again and said, "Yes. Pentex Oil is one of the holdings of Transcontinental Enterprises. Alfonso Birelli is chairman of the board."

"Son of a bitch," said Wormsley and put down the phone. He stared at Schilotz and said, "There's a real big fish involved in this thing. Pentex belongs to Transcontinental Enterprises and Transcontinental Enterprises belong to Alfonso Birelli."

"Alfonso Birelli?" echoed Schilotz. He was on far too low a rung of the State Department ladder to have even heard of the name, but he pretended otherwise since Wormsley had referred to a "big fish" being involved.

"Yes," said Wormsley. "We're going to have to handle this as if it were dynamite." He paused and Schilotz wondered why people referred to dynamite in the age of nuclear fission. He had that kind of mind. It flitted, bird-like, from twig to twig on even the most pressing occasions.

Wormsley rested his elbows on his desk and clasped his hands so close to his face that he was talking through his thumbs. "There must be some reason why Birelli cut the fuel supply to Grand Fenwick," he said. "There's no question but that it was done on his instruction. Nothing happens in the whole Birelli empire that he doesn't know about. Nothing. The amount of fuel involved is insignificant. It wouldn't have the slightest effect on the world supply. But by cutting it he has managed to provoke a crisis not in a town or a city or a state but in a nation—because Grand Fenwick is a nation—and a most extraordinarily unpredictable nation.

"He has a reason then, and that reason, in some way I don't see at this moment, may involve the United States in serious difficulties."

He stopped, pulled open the top right-hand drawer of his desk and checked to ensure that the tape recorder was not running. Ever since Watergate, which had occurred during his junior year at Columbia, he had been very careful about what was recorded. He wouldn't want a word on any tape that referred to so powerful a figure as Alfonso Birelli.

He looked sharply over at Schilotz and said, "What's your reaction?"

Schilotz remembered that part of his horoscope which had advised him to express himself. He cleared his throat and said boldly, "I still think that all we have to do is see that Grand Fenwick gets the fuel it needs. The amount, as I said, is so small the government can supply it from its own stocks if there are some difficulties with the French company."

"That would be to lock horns with Birelli," said Wormsley. "You don't lock horns with Birelli, particularly not in an election year. You don't seem to be getting the point."

"If Birelli is behind this as you think," said Schilotz, "I don't see what he can achieve. What effect can it have on the world at large if someone puts the squeeze on Lilliput?"

"Well for starters," Wormsley explained, "you have the announcement over the media that the world fuel crisis is so acute—though played down for the time being—that a huge oil company had to cut the little Duchy of Grand Fenwick to twenty gallons of gasoline a month or whatever.

"Then people start thinking that the squeeze will affect the little guys first but they're going to feel it themselves. Then the public gets restless on the fuel issue and you have a few congressional committees investigating the whole thing with the usual charges of profiteering by importers, producers, shippers, refiners and distributors.

"Then you get panic buying and the price of oil soars. That's just for starters. And remember that guy Birelli wrote the book on how to pull the strings in full view of the public. I haven't even touched on the impact on the election."

Schilotz was impressed. All that from a few gallons of oil? Imagination. It was something he didn't have and it was the reason that Wormsley, and not he, headed up the Central European Division.

"You may be right," he said slowly. "But if it's that big, don't you think we ought to talk to the Secretary about it?" He paused and passed his plumpish hand over his fair boyish hair again. He'd been bold. He'd expressed himself. Now he began to feel nervous. "On the other hand," he added, "if it's just a bureaucratic mix-up and we bring it to the attention of the Secretary, it will reflect badly on the department."

"Where Birelli is concerned, there are no bureaucratic mix-ups," Wormsley said.

"We could suggest that the Secretary mention the matter casually to Birelli," Schilotz explained. It was plain to him now that Birelli was a big enough man to be on speaking terms with the Secretary. "The Secretary might smoke something out of him."

Wormsley looked again at the letter with "Please advise" written on it in Hannigan's firm italic script.

"Thanks for your input," Wormsley said, dismissing Schilotz with scarcely a glance. He then pressed a button which would summon his secretary, Miss Rita Molino, to his desk. He had an important memo to dictate.

CHAPTER

6

The kite which Dr. Kokintz had made for Katherine de Mountjoy, great-granddaughter of the Count, didn't work very well. He had made several models for her, each an improvement on the other. The first was of the sort he had flown himself as a boy, a pair of light, crossed sticks forming an axis, firmly bound at the center, and one longer than the other. The four ends of the sticks were united by string, and the whole structure enveloped in a sheet of newspaper glued to the string with a paste made of flour. Provided with a tail of twisted pieces of paper, the kite worked well enough for Kokintz but Katherine had trouble flying it. It got caught in a tree and was wrecked and Katherine was in tears until Kokintz told her he would make her another.

He made several, each an improved model, but some got caught in a tree and others suddenly nosedived and were smashed on the ground.

"It's quite a problem," said Kokintz to the little girl. "Come help me feed the birds and we'll design a kite together that will not be afraid of trees or the ground. What do you have in your pockets?"

He noticed that her pockets were bulging.

Katherine took out a grubby handkerchief, a mechanical mouse, two pencil stubs, a piece of string with a lot of knots in it, a piece of funny putty and half a bar of candy.

The candy bar was pretty firmly united with the putty, but she pulled them apart. It was chocolate-coated, the center being of toffee.

"Want a bite?" she said, holding it out when she had cleaned the greater part of the funny putty off.

"Yes," said Kokintz and bit off a piece. It tasted just as it had more than sixty years ago when he was a boy. He wondered why it had been so long since he had bought himself a candy bar. He had been busy; busy with the nature and significance of matter. But in all that business he should have left time for a candy bar. "Thank you," he said.

"I like toffee best," said Katherine taking a bite herself. "But sometimes they only have that mushy raspberry stuff in the middle."

"It's all sugar," said Kokintz, and his mind started to toy with the structure of the carbohydrate called sugar. "C six, H 12, O six," he said aloud, which he often did when he was talking to himself. "C six H 12 O six."

"Is that something to do with the kite?" asked Katherine. "It's icky."

But Kokintz wasn't listening. It was a long long time since he had exercised his mind on the pleasing problems of the carbohydrates, not in fact since the days of his schoolboy chemistry. So when he and Katherine had tended to the birds together and he had made her another kite, he asked her for another piece of candy.

He cut it off neatly with a spatula and put it in a test tube and busied himself setting up a series of flasks and retorts, pipettes and water jackets. The end result looked vaguely like an oil refinery but made of glass. When Kokintz had everything to his satisfaction, Mountjoy entered the laboratory.

"Ah," he said viewing the apparatus. "Getting to work, eh? The energy problem."

Kokintz peered at Mountjoy over the rims of his glasses, but it was plain from the expression in his eyes that he hadn't really heard him.

"It's a piece of candy bar," Kokintz said. "Chocolate outside and toffee inside."

"Candy bar?" Mountjoy cried. "What the devil has that got to do with the energy crisis?"

"Tweedledum and Tweedledee," Kokintz said. "That perhaps is the key. It's very curious."

"What is all this nonsense?" demanded Mountjoy and Kokintz finally emerged from the fog and seemed surprised to find Mountjoy in his presence.

" 'Tweedledum and Tweedledee set out to fight a battle,' " he recited. "Fructose and glucose. Only they're not fighting—at least there is no evidence that they are. They have the same atomic content—six carbon atoms, twelve hydrogen atoms and six oxygen atoms. But they are not put together in the same way, though each is a simple sugar. Fructose takes no part in the development of animal tissue, but glucose plays a huge part. Fructose and glucose are equally important in the metabolism of vegetable matter. But fructose seems to have some part to play in the life of certain bacteriological cells. One should be able to play tricks with them. Tweedledum and Tweedledee."

"Pray may I ask once more what has all this to do with the energy problem?" said Mountjoy.

Kokintz looked mildly at the Count.

"That is not a very good question," he said. "It is like asking Columbus when he set sail, as he thought, for India, what his voyage had to do with the erection of skyscrapers in New York. He knew nothing of New York, nothing of America and nothing of skyscrapers.

"Yet his voyage produced, as a by-product, all these things. I am going to take a voyage of exploration myself and my ship will be a piece of your great-granddaughter's candy bar, which is a form of sugar.

"Sugar is one of the most common substances on earth. Sugars are very easy to produce chemically and there are hundreds of sugars. But one natural sugar only—glucose—is the form most common to life on earth. Why glucose? With the same atomic content one can produce sixteen kinds of primary sugars by rearranging the atomic placement, and eight of them are mirror images of their partners. But one always comes back to glucose as the favorite of nature, though for what reason we do not know. If you were to ask me what is the most important biochemical process in the whole universe I would say without hesitation, the ability of plant life to receive energy from the sun and by photosynthesis transform it into living matter." He paused to reflect. "I put that broadly," he said. "But to my mind this is the greatest of all the wonders in the universe."

Mountjoy was not listening. Kokintz was off on one of his scientific diversions again. "So many mysteries," he said and started speculating why all twenty amino acids known to man should polarize light to the left. Fructose polarized light to the left also, but glucose polarized it to the right. So nature knew how to perform that trick, but preferred to make amino acids, on earth at least, all left-handed so to speak.

Mountjoy departed and entering the courtyard of the castle came face to face with his great-granddaughter Katherine in a towering rage and with a broken kite in her hand.

"The stupid thing fell on its head again," she said.

The two confronted each other. He politely asked Katherine not to visit Kokintz with her broken kite, stressing the importance of what the scientist was working on.

"What about my kite?" demanded Katherine, holding up the bedraggled wreck, her rage now turned to tears of frustration and misery.

"Let Grandpa fix it," Mountjoy said.

Katherine eyed him with deep suspicion. In her memories of him, and although she was but seven these seemed very long memories indeed, she had never known him to fix anything. He just ordered other people to do so.

"You know how to make a kite?" she asked.

"Certainly," said Mountjoy. This was a lie, but it was told not for the sake of lying but for the sake of keeping Kokintz at work on whatever he was working on. It was, then, a diplomatic device rather than a lie and so entirely forgivable.

Katherine said nothing and Mountjoy knew he had to follow up the lie with a bribe. Shoddy diplomacy. He disliked it but nonetheless it was necessary if Grand Fenwick and the world were to be spared the economic wreckage which would result from the fuel crisis. "You can have tea with me," he said. "Tea and toast."

"Gooseberry jam?" asked Katherine, for she had learned her great-grandfather's wisdom in never accepting the first offer, however attractive, lest more could be obtained.

"Gooseberry jam," said Mountjoy.

"All right," said Katherine and the two went, hand in hand, up to the castle and then to his study, where Mountjoy rang for tea. When Meadows arrived and had been told to bring an extra cup and lots more toast and some gooseberry jam, Mountjoy went to a beautifully inlaid cabinet in which for his convenience (for he liked to write many letters by hand) there was a supply of stationery. He took out a very large, pale-blue sheet of excellent paper made from fine linen. It was his favorite sort. The big sheets he used in addressing presidents and the world's remnant of kings. A smaller size for members of foreign cabinets and smaller sheets still for ambassadors, for he had a well-constructed sense of proportion in such matters.

At the top of the sheet of paper (it was of the king size) in Gothic letters were the words

Duchy of Grand Fenwick

and below this the coat of arms of the Duchy, the double-headed eagle saying "Yea" from one beak and "Nay" from the other.

Below that, written on a scroll and clutched in the eagle's talons was the motto of Grand Fenwick: the single Latin word "Superviveo"—"I survive."

"This should make an excellent kite," he said. And he reflected that he had used the paper in a similar fashion many times before in his diplomatic correspondence.

CHAPTER

7

Peter Wormsley made three drafts of his memo to Kurt Hannigan, presidential adviser, on the subject of the oil supply to Grand Fenwick before he achieved a version with which he was halfway satisfied. Then he shredded all three versions, had a short talk with Secretary of State Thatcher and put a call through to Hannigan's office.

"Wormsley here," he said. "Can you give me a moment for a personal chat? I want to talk about the Grand Fenwick thing."

"What Grand Fenwick thing?" asked Hannigan, who had spent a nerve-wracking day with several representatives of the OPEC countries trying to get them to agree to increase production and keep the price of oil at thirty dollars a barrel. He had failed dismally.

"The reduction in oil supplies," said Wormsley. "Right at this moment I don't think anything should be committed to paper."

Hannigan recalled the memoir from the Count of Mountjoy and wondered whether some form of insanity, akin to the South Sea Bubble of the eighteenth century, had taken possession of the chancelleries of the world. Here was a nation as powerful as the United States entangled in negotiations with tiny countries like Iraq and Oman and Yemen—and Grand Fenwick—while the colossi of the world, Red China and the Soviet Union, peered on from afar. Well, maybe it wasn't like the South Sea Bubble but more like Gulliver in Lilliput.

"Look," said Hannigan. "I've had one hell of a day and I'm about to go home, drink three ice-cold martinis, take two Dalmanes and go to bed. Can't it wait until morning?"

"No, sir," said Wormsley. "We must reply to Grand Fenwick almost immediately; otherwise they have the right to void their treaty with us—and that involves setting them at liberty to do what they wish with the Q-bomb."

"Have you spoken to the Secretary about this?" Hannigan asked.

"Yes, sir," said Wormsley. "He said I should take it up personally with you. It's an executive, not a policy matter, in his view."

"All right," said Hannigan. "Come on over. I'll see you in half an hour."

As a result of having written three memos on the subject, Wormsley had the main points of what he wanted to say clearly in his mind and was able to present them succinctly to Hannigan, who stared out of the window of his office, tapping his teeth with a pencil, all the time Wormsley was talking.

When he had done, Hannigan said, "I don't see what

all the fuss is about. It's obviously a mix-up. Ship the oil and prepare a letter of apology for the President's signature."

"What about Birelli?" Wormsley asked. "The indications are that the Grand Fenwick supply was radically reduced—cut off, you might say—at his express instructions. His support of the administration in the coming elections is—er, critical."

"What do you mean by 'indications'?" asked Hannigan.

"Well, the Secretary had a casual conversation with him, and he said that in view of the growing world shortage, with the need (not yet announced) that international quotas have to be imposed to reduce consumption, bring the price of oil down again and combat inflation, Grand Fenwick would not get any oil at all. Actually if the quota as now worked out were strictly applied, Grand Fenwick would get about a gallon and a half of gasoline a month, and about two pints of fuel oil."

Hannigan considered this, all the time staring out of the office window as if somewhere outside his office and beyond the White House grounds lay the answer to the problem.

"We're seeing more in this thing than there is," he said at last. "Someone in Birelli's organization obviously had the figures run through the computer and started imposing the Pentex quotas without even thinking of what they were doing. There's no need for a quota for places like Grand Fenwick. Christ, if they increased their consumption three hundred percent, it wouldn't have the slightest effect on the world oil picture. This is just the result of someone sitting down before a computer and carefully removing his head first. It's a phenomenon which is becoming more and more common. I'll tell the

Navy to get the gasoline and oil to Grand Fenwick until the Pentex supplies can be restarted. Have that letter of apology from the President to Grand Fenwick on my desk tomorrow morning and that's all there is to it."

When Wormsley had gone Hannigan reached for the telephone and called Caleb Abrams, Secretary of the Navy. The Secretary was not in his office, but his executive assistant, Tom Fielding, took the message.

"Two hundred gallons of unleaded gasoline and one hundred of fuel oil to be sent immediately to Grand Fenwick?" he said. "An emergency? All right, sir. We'll fly it there right away. Delivery once per month until canceled? Got it."

He put down the telephone and speculated which of the United States Navy installations throughout the world bore the code name Grand Fenwick. The name seemed vaguely familiar but he couldn't place it, so he went to the console and typed out a question for the Navy memory bank. Back on the sheet of glass above the console came the answer.

"GRAND FENWICK CODE NAME FOR GROUP A 247 DL COORDINATES 80 N 80 W ELLESMERE ISLAND ARCTIC OCEAN."

"Poor bastards," said Fielding. "They must be freezing." The Navy plane with the oil supplies was on its way to the frigid twilight of the roof of the world within an hour, where a dozen technicians, warm as toast in their underground dwellings, were studying meteorological conditions and incidentally keeping a close radar watch for the launching of hostile intercontinental ballistic missiles.

A week later the Count of Mountjoy, who had had his last hot bath several days earlier, received a letter from the President of the United States saying that it was entirely the result of an oversight that oil supplies to Grand Fenwick had ceased and that he had personally given orders for their immediate resumption. A new and ample supply of gasoline and heating oil could be expected by air immediately.

"By air?" said Mountjoy. "Where are they going to land it?" The nearest airport was Besançon, many miles from the Duchy, from which delivery would have to be made by road. But it pleased him that the supplies were being flown and he daily awaited the arrival of the tank trucks. But when, after two weeks, not a drop of oil had reached Grand Fenwick, his patience was exhausted and he summoned a special meeting of the Council of Freemen to discuss the situation.

"What we are presented with," he told the assembled members, "is a flagrant and I might say cynical disregard of an important clause of the treaty between this Duchy and the United States of America. Members may examine at their leisure the correspondence which has passed between me and the President of the United States. They will see that despite my several complaints and the specific promise of the President to implement that important clause under which it is their duty to supply this nation with both gasoline and fuel oil, the United States has failed to do so.

"It is my duty then to bring to the attention of the House that the aforesaid treaty is now null and void and no longer binding on the Duchy of Grand Fenwick as of this day."

"What about the Arabs?" asked Bentner.

Mountjoy fixed him with a look of icy disdain.

"I fail to see what the Arabs have to do with this," he said.

"Well, can't we get enough oil to heat your bath water from the Arabs?" Bentner replied. "That's what it's all about, isn't it?" And he looked about at his colleagues on the opposition benches, who were chuckling with delight.

Mountjoy waited for the chuckles to subside, placed his monocle in his eye and said, "I had hardly thought it would ever be necessary, in this august assembly, to point out that treaties are not personal arrangements between individuals but solemn compacts agreed between nations, and on their sanctity rests the international intercourse of the civilized world. They govern the conditions of that intercourse and of trade and of friendship between nations, and if one is allowed to be broken without firm action, then none may be held to be of solid worth and nothing but chaos can result. They have nothing to do with hot bath water."

Bentner seemed subdued, but only for a moment. "It's all very well to say that it's got nothing to do with bath water," he said, "but we'll all be in plenty of hot water of another kind if we break that treaty. About the first thing I can see happening is the United States will cut off the market for our wine and wool. All very well to say that we can find markets elsewhere. Maybe so. But not without some trouble, and why upset the arrangement that stands at the present time?

"I'm not even going to talk about the Q-bomb, which is covered by that same treaty. We're international guardians of the Q-bomb, but many's the time I've wished someone would take that dratted thing and explode it somewhere in space. Hens haven't been laying at all well these past several years. Got three eggs last week double-yolked and the shells were pinkish."

"What," asked the Count of Mountjoy, "have your hens got to do with the Q-bomb?"

"I think it's leaking radiation," Bentner said. "That's what it's got to do with the Q-bomb. Ted Weathers, that lives in the cottage nearest the castle where the bomb is kept, was telling me the other day that he gets headaches and trembling spells and sometimes can't see properly."

"It isn't closeness to the castle that produces these interesting symptoms in Ted Weathers," said Mountjoy, "but closeness to the tavern." This brought a roar of laughter, the Grey Goose being a favorite haunt of Ted Weathers. When order was restored Mountjoy told the House that the honorable Leader of Her Grace's Loyal Opposition seemed to have missed the point of the whole debate.

"I find I have to emphasize that it is not a matter of Grand Fenwick breaking its treaty with the United States. It is a matter of the United States having already voided its treaty with Grand Fenwick. I have called this special session to inform members of this fact. The treaty is already null and void despite every effort on my part to preserve it. Its terms have been violated, I repeat, not by ourselves but by the United States. We have no treaty with them as matters stand at this moment.

"Members are no doubt aware of the recent talks between the United States and the Soviet Union on the limitation of strategic armaments. They are popularly known as the SALT talks. We have never been invited to take any part in them, though as possessors of the quadium bomb we are certainly an atomic power, and by no means a minor atomic power.

"The violation of the treaty by the United States leaves us free to open SALT talks of our own with whatever countries may be interested. With the permission of the House, I propose to open such talks."

At this there was a storm of protest which the Speaker had some difficulty in bringing under control.

"The opening of talks does not necessarily mean the concluding of agreements," said Mountjoy. "We live, gentlemen, in a world swept by hurricane forces. I refer not merely to the proliferation of atomic armaments of horrendous potential; I refer equally to economic weapons which can cause innocent nations to wither and fall into the pit of poverty. I refer to the prospect of unemployment for millions of people, to the destruction of currency and with it the destruction of the value of the work of honest men. I refer to the chaos of world economic collapse. And that is the threat which lies before us all at this moment in world history.

"With that threat plainly in view, we in Grand Fenwick must not shirk our duty to mankind in every part of the world. I have given the matter much thought and have formed certain tentative plans. I will ask the indulgence of the House in not insisting that I reveal them now. I ask only, as an initial step, the assent of members to my proposal that we open SALT talks—that is, talks concerned with the future of the Q-bomb—of our own, without specifying for one moment with what country or countries they are to be conducted."

Nobody knew what to say to this. Things seemed to be getting entirely out of hand. Everybody had been chuckling earlier in the meeting about Mountjoy's determination to get a hot bath. Now world economic collapse had been thrust before them, in some way linked to nuclear disarmament and the terrible bomb which, detonated, could destroy whole continents, in the conservative opinion of Dr. Kokintz.

In the silence the Speaker glanced from one side of the little House of Freemen to the other—from Bentner, Leader of the Opposition, to Mountjoy, leader of the Government. He was feeling uneasy, sensing that a moment had arrived which would leave its mark on the history of the Western powers and indeed the world. But he had his duty to do.

He passed the tip of his tongue over thin lips and picked up the goosequill pen which lay on the desk before him. He examined the goosequill, admiring the grace of its construction, the flow of the vanes up the central ridge, the lightness and strength of the whole design. It was a thing without voice or intelligence, and it was entirely at peace with itself. Mankind . . . He stopped the thought, for the business of the House must be put in hand.

"Does the Prime Minister wish to put the matter in the form of a motion?" he asked.

Mountjoy looked about the chamber. The members were taken aback, puzzled, unsure. He did not need half a century of parliamentary experience to know that they were not with him and the motion would fail.

"I respectfully suggest that the Speaker adjourn the House at this time to reconvene in two hours," he said.

The motion to adjourn was passed without dissent and Mountjoy tapped Bentner on the shoulder as they left the chamber.

"We need to talk, you and I," he said. "Would you be kind enough to join me in my study?"

Bentner scratched his head. He couldn't remember ever having won a discussion with Mountjoy, but he had to admit that the Count was a knowing old fox and was often right. In any case, he could not enlighten the members of his own party on what was afoot until Mountjoy had enlightened him.

"No politics?" he said.

"No politics," said Mountjoy. "The matter is too big for politics. It calls for a high order of statesmanship on both our parts. I would be glad of your advice, in fact, after I have laid a few things before you."

"All right," said Bentner. "But let's talk facts and not just suspicions of facts."

"That I promise," said Mountjoy and led him to his study.

CHAPTER

8

"My dear Bentner," said Mountjoy when the two were seated, "I have been guilty of a parliamentary error in not confiding in you before discussing the question of what I have called SALT talks openly in the House. I intended no offense. I did what I thought was right. I was quite wrong."

"Never mind that," said Bentner, wondering what Mountjoy was going to try to put over on him. "What is it you have to say?"

"I have been doing a great deal of thinking and making some extensive private inquiries on the energy shortage, which has resulted in our own meager supplies of needed oil being drastically reduced," said the Count. "At first, I confess, I viewed the matter in quite the wrong light. I thought it just a snub by the French company who supplies us—the French being, as you know, ever anxious to belittle our country since it was wrested from their control in 1370 by Sir Roger Fenwick. Their postal service to Grand Fenwick, for instance, is worse than to the smallest village in France.

"I wrote a letter of protest to the French President—ignored, of course. And I wrote also to the President of the United States with the results I have already disclosed in the House. The problem is bigger, however—far bigger —than Grand Fenwick. The oil shortage, although widely viewed as a temporary thing—a mere inconvenience which has motorists in the United States lined up at petrol stations and householders facing a shivering winter in their homes, is, as I hinted in the House, a threat to the whole economy of the Western world.

"A threat, I said. It is more than that. It is to a degree a plot; a plot by quite selfish and shortsighted men to reduce the world supply of oil while pushing the price up as high as it can go. As the price of energy goes up, so the price of everything energy produces goes up. Wages follow prices, and the oil magnates who are behind this plot make double profits. They produce less. They get more for what they produce."

Bentner sighed. Whenever anybody mentioned inflation to him he thought of balloons, which, overinflated, must burst. The only part of the statement with which he entirely agreed was that the oil companies, being big business and therefore necessarily evil, were out to profiteer from the labor of the working man. That made basic sense to him.

Reflecting on this essential characteristic, as he saw it, of big business, he said, "What's new about that?"

"What's new about it, my dear friend of the working-man," said Mountjoy, "is that this manipulation of the major source of energy in our society, producing massive inflation, will also produce in the end massive unemployment, massive destruction of the value of money, and massive erosion of the life savings and pensions of those who toiled away their lives only to find themselves on retirement facing living conditions which would have driven their grandparents to revolution.

"More than that. Standards of living all over the Western world will come tumbling down even for those who are earning what are thought to be good wages. Goods of every kind will become scarcer—first the nonessentials and then the more essential goods. Finally the world will find itself living at the standard of the eighteen-eighties. That is it in a nutshell. That is the threat to society which we face today, not the threat of extermination in a nuclear holocaust but the eradication of all the social progress we have made in the last century."

"Wait a moment," said Bentner. "There's sources of energy other than oil."

"Why, so there are," replied Mountjoy. "But every one of them is likely to turn out to be every bit as expensive as oil is now. Coal may not be mined at the prices available in the nineteen-thirties, however plentiful it may be. Its transportation to the place where it is to be used is an enormous financial burden. As for solar energy, I have questioned Kokintz and he points to the fact that one major difficulty is the storage of energy derived from the sun. Not to mention the fact that in more northern countries what little would be available from that source might light and heat a few homes (given a method of storage) but would not serve to power industry. I am by no means an expert. Indeed I doubt that there are any experts, but it seems that an entirely new source of energy

—abundant, cheap and physical—capable of storage without resorting to batteries and methods of transmission which we do not possess, must be found. "I have spoken to Kokintz about it, and he is working on the problem—"

"Last time I saw him," said Bentner, "he was working on a kite with your great-granddaughter. In his lab he had a whole mess of stuff. I think he's making candy bars—"

"I know. I know," said Mountjoy, irritated. "He has his peculiarities, but he is the one man in the world who can be relied upon to discover a new boundless and cheap source of energy. But to return to the problem—the problem of the present and growing shortage of oil energy, which represents a sort of energy bomb threatening the whole of civilization—it is time that Grand Fenwick took a hand. We produce no oil ourselves. We have a vast experience of international affairs. We are in a sense called upon by humanity, as a neutral in the energy field, to save them in a crisis brought about by other nations whose vision is limited to their own national interests. It is for that reason, my dear Bentner, that I proposed to the House that we open SALT talks of our own."

"I can't see what SALT talks have to do with it," said Bentner. "I can't see it at all."

"Absolutely nothing," said Mountjoy airily. "They will merely provide me with a diplomatic weapon which I can use in negotiations aimed at defusing the energy bomb which now threatens the world."

"What kind of negotiations?" asked Bentner, now highly suspicious.

Mountjoy eyed him closely for a moment. Basically the man wasn't a fool. On the other hand, he had no flair for diplomacy whatever and his political creed, if he had such a thing, could be summed up in the sentence, "Trust no one with a white collar."

"Let us examine the position of the oil-producing nations of what used to be called the Persian Gulf," said Mountjoy. "They have a huge percentage of the world's oil supply. In the matter of oil resources they have the whip hand. But they are squeezed between two powers— the United States and the Soviet Union, which is of course the more threatening and has in recent times become actively threatening.

"They are not without armament. Indeed, they have armament of the most modern kind. I suspect that if warfare were limited to nonnuclear arms, they might be able to put up a good showing, at least for a while. But they do lack nuclear weapons. And it is in this area that we may be of service to them."

"Are you talking about giving the Q-bomb to the blooming Arabs?" asked Bentner.

"I'm not talking at present about giving the Q-bomb to anybody," replied Mountjoy. "I am suggesting only that the prospect of giving the Q-bomb to what you call the blooming Arabs may produce a power equilibrium leading to an international agreement covering oil supplies and prices which would avert the energy crisis which threatens to engulf us all. It is my purpose to bring about such an agreement."

"Look here, Mountjoy," said Bentner, "there are plenty of other statesmen in the world, economists and so forth, who are probably anxious to bring about such an agreement without us meddling in the thing. Wine and wool. That's Grand Fenwick's business and nothing else."

"My good Bentner," said Mountjoy, "if this crisis persists, who do you think is going to have the money to buy our wine and our wool? They are both what are called by the vulgar luxury items, though how a man may get through life without a decent suit of worsted and a wine of some nobility on his table, I do not know. To be sure, we have sold our wool through the centuries, but that was before the introduction of artificial fabrics—drip-dry clothing for drip-dry minds.

"As to your charming belief that there are other statesmen, economists and so forth in the world, anxious to bring about an equitable agreement on oil supplies and prices, I ask you only to look at the record. These very statesmen and these same economists have produced exactly the opposite. Shortsightedly grabbing for themselves, juggling their figures and their prognostications to suit their national interests, they have produced the present imbroglio, with the might of Russia and the might of the United States confronting each other across the silent and peaceful deserts of Arabia, Iran and Afghanistan."

It took a great deal more argument on the part of Mountjoy, but in the end Bentner reluctantly agreed with the Count.

"We, you and I," said Mountjoy, rising when the talk was done, "hold the fate of Western society in our hands. We will keep in the closest touch with each other, but let us not disclose to the others the substance of what has passed between us."

"So long as it doesn't hurt the sales of wine and wool," said Bentner, and the Count, leading him from the study, reflected that Bentner would probably bring up the subject of wine and wool before the throne of God on Judgment Day.

CHAPTER

9

The motion acknowledging the voiding of the treaty with the United States and permitting the Count of Mountjoy a free hand in opening what were loosely called SALT talks with such nations as he thought fit was passed without further debate in the Council of Freemen.

The immediate result which the Count had anticipated was not forthcoming, however.

He had hoped for wide media coverage and a panicked reaction from the United States and the Soviet Union. He got none. A press release was prepared and sent out by GFNS—the Grand Fenwick News Service. It went third-class mail and wound up in the wastepaper baskets of the various news editors who received it. A television camera crew did arrive in Grand Fenwick a week later, but it turned out they were doing a documentary on the various surviving principalities in Europe and they were not at all interested in the momentous decision taken by the Council of Freemen.

No nation in the world had thought the Duchy of sufficient importance to establish a consulate within its borders, so there was no official report of the news from embassies and consulates to any government, although Mountjoy, of course, undertook to officially inform the foreign departments of the United States, Great Britain, France, the Soviet Union and other affected nations of the development. However, so great was the daily inflow of diplomatic correspondence and reports into these various departments that the Grand Fenwick statement was lost from sight.

Mountjoy concluded that he was not being taken seriously—always a tremendous handicap in the little nation's dealing with other countries. There was now no heating oil at all in Grand Fenwick. But far away in the North, within the limits of the Arctic Circle a group of scientists, radar operators and military men, receiving a large and unasked-for supply flown in by the United States Navy, concluded that some emergency loomed ahead, that future shipments were likely to be interrupted, and decided to severely ration their use of oil. They then joined the rest of the world in the big shiver, which was just commencing.

Bentner was greatly relieved that nothing at all happened and congratulated himself that in going along with the Count, he had run no real risks. The world would take care of its own problems and for the time being at least, sales of wine and wool were not to be threatened. On reflection he decided that the fuel shortage might actually increase wool sales, warmer clothing being likely to be widely sought all over the northern hemisphere, and invested some of his capital in a hundred Southdown sheep to add to his not inextensive flocks.

Gloriana, who had of course been informed of the vote, was worried. As Duchess it was not her job to interfere in politics or even the foreign affairs of the country. She had no political power, but she had enormous prestige and could gently advise on critical matters when she felt her advice might be needed.

This, she felt, was just such an occasion and so she joined the Count for tea once more in his study.

"Bobo," she confessed when she had poured tea for the two of them, "I'm getting a little nervous about the way things are going. I don't understand the SALT talk thing but I hope you are going to be very careful and not let that wretched bomb fall into the wrong hands. Did Dr. Kokintz fix it, by the way? The last I heard of it, it wouldn't work because of some spring or other he had made for its insides with a hairpin."

"That detail has not yet been attended to," said Mountjoy. "But it can be at any time. No, Your Grace, I do not intend to let the Q-bomb fall into the wrong hands. But, as I have explained to Bentner, the threat that it might gives me some needed diplomatic leverage."

"Well, that's nice to know," said Gloriana. "But I'm worried about the people in the Duchy. The power station has closed down so everybody has had to go back to lanterns and candles for illumination. None of the water heaters work, of course, the washing machines are useless and people are having to scrub clothes by hand again.

"Lots of them don't know how to do it, so I've arranged for lessons to be given them by old Mrs. Tanner, who still has a washboard and a tub that she never gave up. But it's dreadfully hard on everybody—particularly the women.

It takes a whole day to do laundry, and then it has to be dried on clotheslines like in the old days. And there's all the ironing. The only thing that is better is the bread. Tom Westfield has gone back to using his old charcoal-fired ovens. The bread's scrumptious. But everything else —everything has just gone backward. Are you sure the Americans aren't just making some kind of mistake? I mean, I really can't see any reason why they won't send the oil to us. They're not vicious. But maybe it's just hard for them, with all the millions of things they have to handle, to remember to send oil through that French company to Grand Fenwick."

"I have a letter from the President assuring me of the resumption of oil supplies," said Mountjoy. "And the prospect of their having made a mistake has indeed occurred to me.

"But we must not look upon this problem from a narrow and selfish point of view. What has happened in Grand Fenwick is what, to a greater or lesser extent, the whole world is threatened with. We are now enduring a sample of the sufferings which lie ahead for mankind, though, being an agricultural nation, we will not face the massive unemployment and loss of income which other nations will suffer.

"It is all in all perhaps just as well that we are the first victims of the energy bomb. We could serve as an object lesson to the world, but the world refused to take any notice of us. We are the microcosm that portends the macrocosm—the tiny sample that shows what the whole will shortly be.

"But we are ignored." He sighed and passed a thin aristocratic hand through his thin aristocratic hair. Not for the first time he reflected on the irony that such a mind as his and such a background as his—extending in his ancestry through several centuries of diplomatic history—should have to do its work in so tiny a nation, while bunglers, utterly ignorant of the delicacy and foresight demanded in the dealings of nations, were elected to high office in more powerful countries merely because their faces, on television, looked friendly and reassuring.

"The people do not vote for the facts," he said musingly. "They vote for the faces. Appearance has replaced acumen and the whole world has become a nursery full of children, reassured by kindly pictures."

"You're dreaming, Bobo," said Gloriana.

"I was. I beg Your Grace's pardon," replied the Count. "But to return to the matter in hand. Grand Fenwick has, by some quirk of fate, been elected to serve as an example to the world of what lies before it in this energy crisis. The example, as I remarked, has so far been ignored. But it will not be ignored when I make those diplomatic moves to which I have already referred. At that time, I believe, the world will give us attention—look at what has happened to us and listen to us."

"But I expect everybody is working on the problem of finding and producing more oil," said Gloriana. "I don't see that anything we have to say will help with that."

"To the problem of increased production I do not propose to address myself at this time," said Mountjoy. "It is the problem of equitable distribution and equitable pricing which must be solved immediately. Your Grace may not be aware of it, but my own studies show that much of the present crisis as regards price results from the deliberate actions of the oil magnates. They have bought oil from the OPEC countries at one price and sold it at a greatly inflated price. It is not surprising then that the OPEC countries should decide, by raising the price themselves, to cut out much of this unwarranted profit. Greed has always been bad for business, but it is surprising how long it takes businessmen to learn this lesson. Their creed has been to charge as much as the market will bear. They may do that with ready-baked pies, but they may not do it with oil, which is the very blood of industry.

"I think, Your Grace, if you will leave the matter in my hands, we may look for an international conference on this question to be held in Grand Fenwick in the near future."

"But," Gloriana asked, "how could we provide hot water and heat and transport for the delegates?"

"We won't," said Mountjoy. "That will be an important aspect of the conference."

A few days after this encounter, Mountjoy, who had now a shocking head cold in common with a large proportion of the Duchy's population, received an unexpected telephone call from Paris.

"This is Mr. Birelli's secretary," said the caller. "Mr. Birelli is in Paris and wishes to call to see you."

"Who, may I ask, is Mr. Birelli?" demanded the Count, stifling a sneeze. There was a shocked silence on the line and then Miss Thompson, for it was she who was making the call, said, "Mr. Birelli is chairman of the board of Transcontinental Enterprises, which includes among its holdings Pentex Oil, a company of which you may have heard. He would like to talk to you about the oil shortage."

"Excellent," said Mountjoy. "I suppose he finally got hold of one of our press releases?"

"Press release?" said Miss Thompson, mystified. "I don't think so. Mr. Birelli has urgent reasons for wanting to consult with you. I am afraid I can say nothing further on the telephone."

"When can I expect him?" asked Mountjoy.

"He will be flying from Paris tomorrow in his private plane. I assume it will be possible for him to land in Grand Fenwick?"

"Definitely not," said Mountjoy. "The nearest airport is at Besançon, on French territory. He will have to come the rest of the way, perhaps one hundred and twenty kilo meters, by car. When the speedometer shows one hundred and sixteen kilometers the chauffeur should watch for a side road marked by a grove of beech trees. He should turn left there, otherwise he will miss Grand Fenwick altogether. There was a sign but it has been destroyed. The French, you know."

There was another silence on the line and Miss Thompson said, her voice a trifle unsteady, "Mr. Birelli will come the rest of the way by helicopter. I assume that there is an appropriate landing place?"

"In that case," said Mountjoy, "he should land at the north end of the castle courtyard. If he lands at the south end, he will disturb the cattle. Sours the milk. Try to have the thing come down quietly." With that he hung up and rang for Meadows.

When the butler arrived Mountjoy said, "Have Hitchcomb, Keeper of the Portcullis, paint a large white cross at the north end of the courtyard behind the donjon keep. We're expecting a helicopter tomorrow. Of course the radio station is out and I'm not able to make an announcement to the nation."

He glanced at his watch. It was one-thirty in the afternoon and a Wednesday. The Grand Fenwick *Times,* which came out every Thursday, was probably being printed at that very moment, the flywheel of the press on which it was produced being turned by hand for lack of power. He picked up the telephone, was fortunate to get a free line and asked the operator to connect him to Stedforth, editor of the paper.

"Stedforth," he said, "Mountjoy here. How are you?"

"I've got a hell of a cold."

"So have half the people in the Duchy," said Mountjoy.

"We're running a story about it in tomorrow's edition," said Stedforth. "Calling it Arabian flu. Serve 'em right."

"Look here," said Mountjoy, ignoring this. "I have something I want you to put prominently in the paper."

"Can't," said Stedforth. "Locked her up last night. Got about three hundred run off right now. Won't be able to print over fifty more at the best. Printers are ready to strike. Can't say I blame then. That flywheel's shocking heavy."

"Hang the printers," said Mountjoy. "This is a matter of national concern. A helicopter is to land in Grand Fenwick tomorrow afternoon. It's important that everybody should know about it. This is a friendly visit. We are not being invaded and I don't want anybody shooting arrows at it."

"Tomorrow afternoon?" cried Stedforth. "We won't have the paper folded and ready for delivery until about eleven in the morning. The best thing to do is send people around on bicycles to warn everybody. Even so I'm afraid they can expect a few arrows if they come in low."

"Good God," cried Mountjoy. "Spread the word by messengers? Hang this energy crisis. We've been booted straight back into the Middle Ages. Well, do what you can. It is, as I have said, a matter of national concern. Send some of your circulation people out on bicycles right now."

"Who's going to pay them?" demanded Stedforth.

"I will," snapped Mountjoy and added in tones that Garrick might have envied, "Was ever a nation's fate dependent upon bicycles?"

"Well, the crown of England was lost for lack of a horse," said Stedforth drily and hung up. A few minutes later, half a dozen reluctant bicyclists, representing the total force of the circulation department of the Grand Fenwick *Times*, mounted their machines and cycled reluctantly to the four quarters of the Duchy. Each had been equipped with a megaphone and as they passed farmhouse, hamlet and tiny village, they shouted, "We're not being invaded. Don't shoot at the helicopter." It is the nature of such messages, always at the mercy of air currents, to be garbled. Some got it right. Some got only "Helicopter. We're being invaded." Grandson, sire and grandsire left field, garden plot and vineyard and going to their cottages fetched down their bowstaves from the rafters in which they were stored—six-foot bows of best English yew of the kind that saw service at Crécy, Poitiers and Agincourt.

"Must be them blooming Arabs," they agreed and converged on the castle to practice at the butts in the courtyard beyond the stables.

Meanwhile Mountjoy had gone to inform Gloriana of the unexpected visitor and Gloriana's first question was where Birelli was to be housed.

"In the Acre Tower, of course," said Mountjoy. (All the towers of Grand Fenwick castle were named after towns made famous in the various crusades, to which the Duchy had always sent a contingent, though often enough of only four longbowmen under a man-at-arms.)

"Oh, not the Acre Tower," said Gloriana. "It's so cold and damp there. He'll freeze to death. The tower is right over the moat."

"The Acre Tower would be entirely suitable in the case of Mr. Birelli," said Mountjoy. "He should certainly be given a sample of that which he is bringing to the world."

"I won't hear of it," said Gloriana with surprising firmness. "I do not wish to add to Mr. Birelli's accomplishments the loss of plain courtesy towards a guest. The great disaster to the world would be when we all start losing our manners."

Mountjoy blushed and bowed his head under the rebuke.

"Forgive me, Your Grace," he said. "I was not myself."

"Oh, Bobo," said Gloriana. "Of course I forgive you. I do the same thing myself several times a day. But just where shall we put him? He's got to be warm and cozy and it must be somewhere in the castle."

"The solarium then," said Mountjoy. "Its stained-glass windows face south, as you know, and the play of the colors from the setting sun on the walls and floor is very pretty. There's a good fireplace and a fourposter bed with goosefeather mattress. And he'll have all the privacy he wishes."

That being settled—it was for Gloriana the most important aspect of the visit—she then turned to the purpose of Birelli's mission and Mountjoy, drawing extensively upon speculation and fragments of memory, tried to enlighten her.

"Alfonso Birelli is the czar, if not the mogul, of the oil industry," he said. "I recall something of him now. He is not, I think, in the production end of the industry, which, as Your Grace knows, lies very largely in the hands of the OPEC nations, but rather the purchasing, refining, distribution and marketing aspects. Others pump the oil out of the ground. He buys it and sells it to the world. Not he alone, of course. But he is the major figure in the area of marketing and as such exercises a strong influence, indeed control, over world retail prices.

"I have no doubt that he sells at one hundred percent of the price at which he buys after taking out all his shipping and refining and other expenses. The OPEC nations have raised their prices in order to cut into Birelli's profits. All Birelli has done has been to raise his price to compensate. So the whole thing mounts."

Mountjoy went on talking about the effect of this on inflation, cost of production of goods, closing down of factories, unemployment and even (as he saw it) the collapse of nations. He was in a jubilant mood that such a figure had decided to visit him. Gloriana had no head for such stuff. Mountjoy, plunging on, quite lost himself in his prophecies of a world trying to live with the energy output of the early 1900s, and Gloriana at last interrupted him saying, "Bobo, why should a man as great as he be coming to Grand Fenwick?"

"The answer to that will be provided by Mr. Birelli himself," said Mountjoy. "But I say with some pride that I have baited the trap and he has entered it. I look forward to his visit with the greatest interest. We are on the verge of splendid things."

"Do be careful," said the Duchess.

"I will," replied Mountjoy. "The fate of mankind now rests in my hands." He very much liked the idea.

Down in his laboratory among his birds, Dr. Kokintz had at last devised a kite for Katherine guaranteed not to fall on its head or its tail irrespective of the nature of the wind and air currents. (Mountjoy's attempt had been a failure and Katherine had gone back to the scientist again for help.) It looked like a series of airplane wings, arranged on a stick one below the other, and held together with a very strong glue he had made out of several candy bars, bought at the village store.

He had made something else too—a thickish liquid with a slightly blue tinge to it. It showed no reaction of any kind to all standard tests from litmus paper to electrolysis, including short bursts from the white laser he had devised. An electric current, whatever the voltage, would now not pass through it. It was electrically inert. It had only one peculiar property which excited him and which he had discovered by accident. He had placed a test tube, containing a few drops of this bluish liquid, next to one of the many birdcages with which he was surrounded.

The cage contained a chaffinch. When Kokintz came to feed it, the chaffinch emitted a trill of delight and the test tube rose in the air, circled the room gracefully for a minute and then crashed in smithereens on the floor.

Kokintz squinted through his spectacles at the splinters of glass and then at the chaffinch.

"Bird water," he said. "It seems that I have discovered bird water." Neglecting the chaffinch for the moment, he went to a wall of his laboratory lined with books and tomes of every kind. He took down Hazlitt's "Ultra-sonic Notes of European Wild Birds" and Tu-sin Yung's "Periods of Atomic Particles." He was soon lost in these volumes, and for once in his life he forgot to feed his birds.

CHAPTER

10

Despite the warning of Mountjoy and the added efforts of David Bentner, who had of course been informed of what was to take place, Alfonso Birelli's helicopter was greeted with a thicket of arrows when it landed in the courtyard of the castle. The tires were punctured, several stuck in the underbody, while others glancing off, were smashed to pieces by the rotor. This necessitated the sending of a new rotor (by bus) to Grand Fenwick from Paris.

The astonished Birelli descended from the helicopter to be greeted by Mountjoy, Bentner and a crowd of Fenwickians who shouted "Arabs go home" and "Walk a mile with your camel," for they were free men, accustomed to speaking their minds, and they were convinced, on the solid foundation of rumor, that some Arabian prince was coming to see them, perhaps to buy the castle at some fabulous sum, and fill it with shameless hussies as had been done in Beverly Hills and elsewhere—that also on the solid foundation of rumor.

Birelli, stooping, cleared the arc of the rotors and then standing upright looked about him, a tall gray wolf of a man surveying a flock of healthy, bleating sheep. Only Mountjoy stood as tall as he. The shouting died down as these two—the one an aristocrat of industry and the other a peer of the blood—confronted each other, each the champion of his particular level of society, both of them well above the masses, both of them men who, however heavily beset, gave no quarter.

"Mr. Birelli, I presume," said Mountjoy, who never could rid himself of the formula with which Stanley had greeted Livingstone in his grandfather's time.

"You can call me Al," Birelli replied, reaching out a powerful hand and eyeing the other keenly.

"Mountjoy," said the Count as if he were displaying his escutcheon with his coat of arms (wyvern argent, rampant et regardant on a field, gules). "This is Mr. David Bentner, Leader of Her Grace's Loyal Opposition," he added.

Bentner, who didn't know whether the occasion was formal or not, had compromised in his dress by putting on a pair of striped pants under a corduroy jacket, topping the whole thing with his best bowler hat. He didn't know much about Birelli except that he was a rich and powerful man in the oil business. He had brought with him a gift—a pleasantly made basket in which on a bed of wool lay two bottles of Pinot Grand Fenwick, 1965—a year of considerable unrest about the world which was ameliorated to some degree by a premier grand cru wine from the Duchy.

"Pleasure to meet you, Mr. Machiavelli," he said. "I've

brought a present for you: wine and wool produced in Grand Fenwick and the best in the world."

Birelli smiled, took the basket and decided that the slip-up over names was not an intentional slur.

"May I introduce my secretary, Miss Thompson," he said, motioning her forward. Mountjoy bowed with a grace that brought a smile of pleasure to the sweet motherly face of the hard-as-steel Miss Thompson. Bentner shook her hand warmly. And the crowd stared at the plump and pleasant Miss Thompson in her motherly tweeds and high-necked blouse, then at the striking, handsome figure of Birelli, whose eyes glittered like a stiletto unsheathed in a dark corner, and then at each other.

They were puzzled. If he was a rich, handsome, powerful American, as he now seemed to be, instead of an Arabian prince, why was he traveling with that nice neighborly lady instead of—well, you didn't have to put a word on what he could be traveling with.

"Something's wrong," said Bert Green, owner of the bicycle shop and the gas station, which now had no gas. "There's something about all this that I don't like."

"Mountjoy will get the better of him," said another. "You can see by that look on his face. Pleasant as a scythe blade in the sunlight."

Mountjoy escorted his guests into the castle, where tea was served in the small armory, a chamber of medium size once used to store suits of man and horse armor either in the process of manufacture or in need of repair. Around the walls here and there stood the unused armor, in styles dating from the pot-helmeted chain-mail suits of the crusaders to the fluted graceful plate armor of the Maximilian period. Banners were draped from the walls, gray with the cold breath of the centuries and tattered

95

by the passing of time. Some of the fabric was so thin as to be but a ghostly veil of what was once rich cloth, for the war trophies of Grand Fenwick through the whole of its history were displayed in the small armory. Birelli was startled, looking about, to see among the ancient trophies a new copy of the Stars and Stripes.

"You've got the American flag—Old Glory—hanging here?" he said, pointing.

"Yes," said Mountjoy casually. "We invaded the United States and won. That comes off the Customs Shed in New York. Perhaps you were in college at the time. The history books would hardly have been revised at that date. Indeed I notice some hesitancy about revising them at all. But then history is truth whittled to the national purpose. Do you take sugar? It's orange pekoe."

"I'd sooner coffee," said Birelli.

"Indeed?" said Mountjoy. "We have Brazilian and Nigerian, which I find a trifle better. Which do you prefer?"

"Brazilian for Mr. Birelli," said Miss Thompson, sensing the polite conflict between the two. "One loaded teaspoonful to a cup. He likes it steaming hot." These orders were transmitted to the butler, who, opening a little cupboard set against the wall, wrote the order on a piece of paper and sent it down a shaft elevator to the kitchen a hundred and fifty feet below. The coffee was back in a remarkably short while, for the old-fashioned kitchen range was now in use, fed by blocks of wood, and the gas-powered stove sulked unused in the corner. The advantage of the old kitchen range was that there was boiling water available in kettles and pots at all times.

There was now a round of small talk. Birelli had hoped to be greeted by Gloriana XII and Mountjoy was determined that he would not be. Gloriana was a ruling sovereign; Birelli, whatever his power, a mere merchant. To forestall Gloriana's normal democratic and hospitable tendencies (she had once been delighted to have as her guest in the castle a lady from Kansas City, Kansas, who taught in a real American public school)—to forestall these tendencies Mountjoy had asked her to ride her bicycle into France.

"I don't want you to greet Birelli when he arrives," he said, "and I know that if you stay in the castle you just won't be able to avoid him. It would be better if you aren't in the Duchy at all when he turns up."

"Why, Bobo?" asked Gloriana.

"Just leave it to me," pleaded Mountjoy. "Later on you can perhaps meet him. At an appropriate time. When meeting him would do us all some good."

Gloriana reluctantly agreed to the bicycle ride but was disappointed, for she had never seen a helicopter land. Still Mountjoy usually knew what he was doing so off she went. The Count had agreed with Bentner that he should withdraw from the tea to give Mountjoy time for a preliminary private interview with Birelli in which to sound him out about the object of his visit and take his measure. Bentner was very suspicious about this.

"No secret deals," he said. "Everything above board. That's the way it's got to be."

"Of course no secret deals," said Mountjoy, a trifle impatiently. "I have to sound this man out, privately, before we get down to any serious business. I'm not going to plunge into negotiations right away. Nobody ever does that. You must understand, Bentner, that a person-to-person talk, about a variety of subjects, all the details of which I shall conscientiously lay before you, is likely to bring out much more than if Birelli finds himself con-

stantly in the presence of two people. It's a matter of
. . . er . . ."

"Witnesses," said Bentner. "That's what it's a matter
of."

"Precisely," said Mountjoy smoothly. "Nobody will reveal much of themselves and their aims in the presence
of witnesses—particularly a man of the stature and power
of Alfonso Birelli."

"I thought his name was Machiavelli," said Bentner.

"That's merely his nature," said Mountjoy. "Anyway
I am sure you do understand, my dear Bentner, the need
for the utmost privacy in the first stages. When in the
course of our discussion we get down to more solid matters, be assured you will be fully informed and consulted.
After all, there is nothing I can do as Prime Minister
without the approval of the House of Freemen, where
you, as you are well aware, have a powerful number of
members on your side."

With that Bentner had to be satisfied. He excused himself after a reasonable interval and Mountjoy, who had
been turning his charms on Miss Thompson, suggested to
her that while he would be delighted to have her stay
in the castle, she might be more comfortable in the
Grey Goose tavern. "The castle rooms are very large with
the result that they are also very cold at this time of the
year—at any time of the year in fact. Also facilities for
bathing are extremely limited, whereas at the Grey
Goose, Mrs. Thatcher has a very snug room overlooking
her rear garden and is quite used to arranging the personal facilities required."

Miss Thompson glanced at Birelli and saw him gently
touch the right side of his face which signified an affirmative. So she said she would be delighted to stay at the inn

and Bentner, who had not yet left, agreed to accompany her.

Miss Thompson had of course acquainted herself with all the facts concerning Grand Fenwick before arriving in the Duchy. She knew as much of Bentner's career as she did of Mountjoy and his ancestors, but her reading and inquiries had led her to believe that the Duchess was a person of no importance whatever, a pretty woman with a mind not much above that of an educated child.

She wanted to check this out, for a great part of her worth to Birelli lay in the fact that she checked out everything, not once but several times.

In the short walk from the castle to the inn she asked whether Her Grace was in the castle and Bentner said she had gone on her bicycle into France.

"She may bring back a gallon or two of petrol," said Bentner. "Daimler's been dry now for two days."

"On her bicycle?" said Miss Thompson, genuinely astonished. "To get some gasoline?"

"Oh, I don't know whether she will or not," said Bentner. "But she's got a good head on her and there's a gas station at Sauverne where they're quite friendly. Not all the French are as bad as people say. Just light-headed. You can't rely on them. Italians are worse, though," he added. Miss Thompson received this news in silence, wondering what would be the world reaction if it became known that the ruler of a small European nation had had to go to a foreign country on a bicycle to bring back two gallons of gasoline for her car.

"I understand that you are suffering acutely from the fuel shortage in Grand Fenwick," she said at length.

"Yes," said Bentner. "But I don't know that suffering is the right word. Just between you and me, Mountjoy's put out because he can't get a hot bath and some of the ladies that had washing machines are a bit miffed because they have to do their laundry by hand and hang the clothes out to dry on a line like in the old days.

"But it's an inconvenience really, that's all. If I had my way I'd ban the importation of any kind of foreign fuel into this country. Nothing wrong with wood fires.

"Wine and wool. That's our real riches and that nobody can take away from us. You don't suppose that Mr. Machiavelli would like to place an order—say a hundred bales of prime fleeces—before the price goes up in the autumn?"

"Birelli," said Miss Thompson. "I really don't know. He's not interested in textiles, so far. But you might talk to him about it."

"Probably make all of seven hundred pounds if he was to place an order now," said Bentner. "That's about one thousand four hundred dollars. Not to be sneezed at. Maybe more by summer shearing time—the way the dollar's going down."

Miss Thompson reflected that fourteen hundred dollars might provide her employer with a new suit, shoes and a shirt, and he owned more suits than he could count.

"Well, I'll talk to him if you like," she said in order to head the conversation into more informative areas. "May I ask you a question?" she continued. "Concerning the Duchess?"

"Oh," said Bentner, suddenly full of caution. "Well, I don't know that I can answer any questions about the Duchess. But what did you want to know?"

"I only ask as a woman," said Miss Thompson. "You know how interested we are in women's rights in the United States. I wanted to know whether she has any real say in the governing of the Duchy. Can she forbid things to be done, for instance, or order them to be done?"

"She can and she can't," said Bentner. "All bills passed by the Council of Freemen must be signed by the Duchess before they become law. Now if she were to refuse to sign a bill, then after a short period of time—usually three months, but there's differences depending on the bill—it can come before the Council again. And if the Council or House—they're the same, you know—passes it once more, then it becomes law whether the Duchess has signed it or not.

"So, like I said, she can and she can't. But I've never known her to refuse to sign a bill passed by the Council because she's got a great respect for what the people want and wouldn't ever hold her opinion superior to theirs.

"Now her father, he was of another mind altogether. Real terror, he was. When the Council passed a bill he didn't like, he'd come down and tell them off like they were a set of schoolboys. Made them feel that they'd been personally disloyal to him. Took Mountjoy all the cunning he had to change Duke Robert's mind."

"Mountjoy was Prime Minister in those days?" asked Miss Thompson, surprised.

"Oh, yes," said Bentner. "Of course, there wasn't a Labor Party then—just Liberal. Like in England."

"So Her Grace doesn't actually have the final say in legislation?"

"Well, like I said, she does and she doesn't," said Bentner doggedly. "Laws are sort of made for men, if you know what I mean. Women are able to find a way around them. Nothing illegal, of course. Maybe what they call the feminine mystique. All I can say is that while she's been our sovereign, I can't think of a single thing that's happened in the Duchy that she hasn't agreed with and

I can think of a lot of things that she maybe got started herself."

This gave Miss Thompson much on which to reflect. How conclusive would Mountjoy's talks with her employer be if they were strongly opposed by the Duchess? Had Mountjoy enough charm and mental agility to bring the Duchess around to whatever he himself decided should be done? They arrived at the Grey Goose and Bentner, having introduced Miss Thompson to Mrs. Thatcher, left. Mrs. Thatcher said she had the best bed-sitting-room in the house waiting for her and a nice fire lit.

"If you would be wanting a bath," she said, "give us an hour's notice so we can heat the water. It's the children's turn tonight but I am sure we can arrange everything. Don't be afraid to speak up."

Miss Thompson decided to forgo her bath that day and retired to her cheerful, warm room, her active mind still debating the problem of who was the person to be contended with in this strange little Duchy—the Count of Mountjoy or the somewhat mysterious Duchess Gloriana. She decided she would concentrate on the Duchess and leave Mountjoy to her employer, Birelli. As for Bentner, he could be dismissed. He was plainly a mental lightweight and not worthy of consideration.

CHAPTER

11

Birelli was two days in Grand Fenwick before, in a private meeting with Mountjoy, he got down to the business which had brought him there so urgently. He would have gotten down to it immediately, for that was his nature—the frontal attack backed by detailed planning. But Mountjoy was of another cast of mind, and saw to it that Birelli had no opportunity for a private talk of any importance until he had persuaded the Duchess, returning from her bicycle ride, to go for a week's vacation at Nice—in the worst season of the year.

"Bobo, what are you up to?" demanded Gloriana when he broached this plan to her. "You've never been so mysterious in all the years I've known you."

"Your Grace," said Mountjoy, "it is essential that you be abroad while Birelli is here. He is a man of tremendous power and tremendous influence. In any negotiation, he likes to be sure that he has all the cards in his hand. The only card I have is your absence—his inability to talk to you. I wish to make him feel a little nervous, a little uncertain. I am dealing from weakness against strength. I humbly ask Your Grace's help."

"But I don't see that even if he did talk with me he could achieve anything," said Gloriana. "You know very well I can't make decisions. And it's bound to be raining in Nice at this time of the year. There's nothing worse than standing under a palm tree and shivering in a downpour."

"People like Birelli are never convinced that someone in your position has no power," said Mountjoy. "In that they are quite correct, of course. Your Grace knows how deep is your influence with all your subjects. It would be better for us if you could not be reached, if, at the conclusion of our talks, Birelli was still not sure that he had achieved whatever it is he has in mind."

"What does he have in mind?" asked Gloriana.

Mountjoy gazed for a moment at his beautifully manicured fingernails and said, "I suspect that he intends to use what he thinks is the simpleminded Duchy of Grand Fenwick in his further manipulation of world oil prices. I, on the other hand, hope to use Birelli to strike a blow for mankind."

Gloriana didn't entirely understand this but agreed to spend a few days in rain-swept Nice, and enough gasoline was scraped together, by a bicycle relay to Sauverne, to drive the Daimler down to the airport in France.

With the Duchess out of the way, Mountjoy agreed to a private business session with Birelli, who had soon made the object of his visit clear.

"I have come on a matter of the greatest delicacy and

the most critical importance," he said. "You and I, alone in this ancient castle, hold in our hands the future of the Government of the United States of America and the future of the whole economic complex of the Western world. I might add that it is you, rather than I, who are of the first importance in both these matters."

Mountjoy, despite himself, was impressed. Birelli, he decided, was more astute than he had given him credit for, recognizing, as he obviously did, Mountjoy's worth and potential to the world which had been so often ignored by others.

"You are in need of my advice?" he asked quietly.

Birelli smiled warmly. This was going to be easier than he thought.

"Yes indeed," he replied. "I need your advice and your cooperation. You are the only man in Europe and America to whom I can come and lay bare my thinking and my planning. You are, I know, fully aware of the present energy crisis and you are aware that it is going to get a lot worse in the weeks ahead.

"You are aware too of the factors which have led to this situation—enormously increased oil consumption, limited production, rising costs of drilling, refining, distribution, marketing and so on, coupled with competitive bidding among the consuming nations.

"Saudi Arabia alone has tried to hold the price line at what might be regarded as reasonable. But the whole of the Persian Gulf production fields are now menaced by the Soviet Union, and the possibility—perhaps the probability—of a vast portion of the world's oil supply falling into communist hands now lies bleakly before us."

Mountjoy nodded. There was nothing new in all this for him and he had never forgotten that the publicly proclaimed aim of the Marxists was to bring about the economic collapse of the capitalist system, which could be most readily achieved by the seizure of its major sources of oil.

"You will also be aware that open warfare for the possession of the oilfields of the Persian Gulf must be avoided at all costs by the West. Warfare would result in the destruction of the very oilfields and refineries which both sides—East and West—would regard as the prize of war. It is my belief that the Soviet plan is to overthrow the various sheikdoms from within, to be replaced by rival sheikdoms favoring the communist cause."

At this point Mountjoy began to get a little bored. This, for him, was all elementary stuff. He objected to being lectured on international aims at the grade-school level.

"Yes," he said. "I quite understand all these matters. I have been following them for some time. So did my father."

"Your father?"

"Yes. The problem of the Persian Gulf has existed in one form or another for well over a century—far back into the time when the Arab nations were part of the Ottoman Empire. I hope you will pardon my saying that only the United States finds these problems new, not having had to be bothered with a foreign policy in the Near East until the late nineteen-thirties. But I interrupt. What solution do you see?"

Birelli was taken aback. Nobody had ever treated him in this manner before. He was used to lecturing while others listened—used to outlining plans which were not for discussion but rather were instructions which others must follow.

106

"Well," he said, "I presume that you are agreed with me that nobody dares go to war with the Arab nations since the prize sought would be destroyed in the course of warfare."

The conference was taking place in Mountjoy's study. Mountjoy got up and walked over to a lancet window and looked down a hundred feet into the courtyard below. There at the south end was the helicopter in which Birelli had arrived with Miss Thompson. "How far can those things fly?" he asked.

"What things?" asked Birelli, taken completely by surprise.

"Helicopters," said Mountjoy.

"I don't know," said Birelli, irritated. "I suppose, given gasoline, they can fly as far as anyone wants them to."

"What about that one there?"

"It has a cruising range of seven hundred miles."

"Interesting," said Mountjoy. "Interesting."

"We were talking about the impossibility of war over the Arab oilfields," said Birelli.

"So we were," said Mountjoy. "So we were. It is an interesting theory."

"It's more than a theory. It's a hard fact of warfare," Birelli insisted. "Now to get to the point, if I may. The real problem is to stabilize world oil prices. I frankly admit that more than any other man in the world perhaps, I have been responsible for their continuing rise. And I am not now about to attempt to stabilize prices for the benefit of my incompetent and shortsighted business rivals, who continue to push them up. Prices have gotten to the point where my own profits are being jeopardized. So are theirs, though they refuse to see it at the present time. The margin between purchase cost and sales price is uncomfortably small. The oil world thinks that all that is needed is to reduce supplies, cut down on the amount of gasoline and fuel oil available, and the sales price will automatically soar. To get a higher price for selling less is every businessman's dream. But I am the only man in the oil world who realizes that that dream can turn into a nightmare. It is about to turn into a nightmare."

Mountjoy was listening with but half a mind. He became aware that Birelli was silent and said, "I am not sure that I can see how it would become a nightmare." But he made the statement merely to draw Birelli on, for he had spent quite a while considering the significance of that letter which had been sent to him though intended for Birelli—the letter from the U.S. Secretary of the Interior Benjamin Rustin, containing the phrase "if there is anything you can do to make us look good as the crisis looms, we'll all be grateful."

The "us" in that letter was of course the present administration of the United States, headed by President John Miller. And Birelli, conferring with Mountjoy, was now in the process of making the administration look good—since it seemingly would serve his purpose to have the existing administration reelected.

"It can become a nightmare," said Birelli, "when the supplies of oil become so restricted that, irrespective of present profit to the oil world, they bring about the closing down of so many industries that we in effect are guilty of slaughtering our own customers. We are close, perilously close, to that position now—stockpiling oil at prices that industry cannot afford. And so I have come to you for advice and help."

"I am entirely at your service," said Mountjoy, who

was not at that moment prepared to offer anything, for he had plans of his own.

"What I have in mind," said Birelli, "is the secret purchase of a vast quantity of oil—say two billion barrels—to be released on the world market at a price substantially lower than the existing price. The amount must be huge. I would not tremble at twenty billion barrels. The price differential must be significant. But the impression must be given that this oil comes from an entirely new source, outside of the Arabian fields—a source which is not interested in the amassing of vast quantities of money by the sale of oil, having nothing whatever to spend the money on. In short, the Duchy of Grand Fenwick."

Mountjoy caught his breath in sheer admiration for the man. Such a plan would never have occurred to him, imaginative and experienced as he was. It was a bold plan; perilous in the extreme. Yet handled with assurance and dash, it could scarcely fail.

"By God, sir," he said, "I underestimated you. I thought you some pettifogging account juggler who had risen to the top in the dreary world of commerce. But you actually are a man of genius, worthy to take your place among the statesmen of history." He held out his hand and shook Birelli's warmly.

"You are agreed?" asked Birelli.

"To the hilt," Mountjoy said. "The plan is brilliant, but working it out will take a great deal of consultation between the two of us."

"I have already worked it out," Birelli said. "But of course I will need your approval, and you understand that everything I suggest may be changed if you so desire.

"First we must have the announcement of the location

of a sea of oil, amounting to many billions of barrels, readily accessible and lying below the surface of the Duchy."

"Perne's Folly would be the best location," Mountjoy said.

"Perne's what?"

"Perne's Folly. It's an area of about a quarter of a mile square, wasteland good for no purpose at all, on which oil derricks can be erected cheek by jowl if you wish without the slightest harm to the countryside or the ecology."

"Who was Perne?" asked Birelli.

"Oh, it's a long story and of no significance," said Mountjoy. "He was a French knight, something of an eccentric, who wished to buy land in Grand Fenwick. He was sold the quarter of a mile of wasteland which thereafter was called Perne's Folly. He was actually something of an artist," he added and then was quiet, for he did not wish to say anything more on the subject. "As I say, that land is the very best place for the erection of what do you call them—drilling rigs?" he continued. "And everybody in Grand Fenwick has a curious belief that Perne's Folly contains hidden riches—gold, diamonds, what you will, of which Perne was aware. The perfect spot, in fact."

Birelli was a little puzzled by all this but put it aside as trivial. The two talked on and on until the major aspects of the plan were agreed. The details were to be worked out by Mountjoy in consultation with Birelli if need be.

When Birelli was about to leave, Mountjoy said to him, almost casually, "There are two minor conditions from my side which I would like to be met to conclude our bargain."

"What are they?" asked Birelli.

"I would like the immediate supply—by tomorrow if possible—of sufficient heating oil for me to get a decent hot bath and to supply our small power station here in the Duchy, so that hot water and electric power and light are once more available to our people. Also sufficient petrol for Her Grace's Daimler and my own Rolls. In addition I should like to have the use of that helicopter for say three months."

"Granted," said Birelli.

"I presume that it was at your command that our supply of oil and gasoline was so drastically reduced—I might say cut off—in the first instance," said Mountjoy, "and I presume that this was done so that you could observe in Grand Fenwick the effect of such privation on larger nations."

"It was indeed I who ordered supplies cut off," said Birelli. "But not for the reasons you think."

"Indeed," said the Count. "May I inquire then what were your reasons?"

"Do you really require an explanation?" asked Birelli. "I thought the matter obvious. I wished, my dear Mountjoy, to engage your mind firmly on the oil crisis since your experience in statecraft is without parallel in Europe. I wished to prepare it to receive the plan which we have now agreed. That thought occurred to me when I realized that you had received a letter from the American Secretary of the Interior referring to the coming oil debacle, that your instinct for taking a hand in the direction of world affairs, demonstrated several times previously, might be aroused. I decided that by savagely reducing supplies to Grand Fenwick I could ensure that your instincts were indeed aroused since it would be your bull that was gored. I could then hope for the full cooperation of yourself and your esteemed Duchy in adjusting the situation to some level of sanity."

Mountjoy poured himself and Birelli a glass of Pinot Grand Fenwick and, examining the red transparency of the precious wine with its little glints of gold here and there, reflected with admiration on the brilliance of Birelli. The man was a most talented liar. The cutting of supplies to Grand Fenwick, he decided, was probably a clerical error resulting from some nonsense with a computer. Either that or the known malevolence of the French. When this error had been brought to Birelli's attention (perhaps by the U.S. State Department) he had devised his present plan for a huge oil strike in Grand Fenwick to tumble world prices back to a level of reasonableness and had contrived meanwhile to see that no further oil reached the Duchy.

"Your foresight is beyond peer, Mr. Birelli," he said, raising his glass. "You neglect nothing. I salute you." He put the glass to his lips and reflected with satisfaction that Birelli had neglected one thing.

He had neglected the Q-bomb.

CHAPTER

12

As a first step toward inaugurating the great Grand Fenwick Oil Strike, Mountjoy wrote to the University of Lausanne, Switzerland, asking for the names of two geological graduates who had not done particularly well in their studies. The Swiss, as is well known to all the world, are the most obliging people and the university without demur sent him the names and addresses of two of their students who had just managed to struggle to the eminence of a degree.

Mountjoy then wrote to them both. They were Johannes Dupin and Karl Stampfli, both of Geneva.

He said he wished a geological survey to be made of a particular area of Grand Fenwick and their names had been suggested to him as eminently suitable for the task. The receipt of these letters astonished both Johannes and Karl, who as it happened had been friends at the university and were still friends now that they had been graduated. Johannes was working as a postal clerk and Karl as a conductor on a streetcar.

Johannes was long and thin and red-haired and had a face which was covered with freckles the color of a carrot. Karl was short and fat and had exceedingly black hair, and at the university, being always together, they had been nicknamed Thunder and Lightning.

"This Count of Mountjoy, whoever he is, must be a gifted imbecile," said Johannes when he had received the letter and called on his friend. "I think we had better reply that we are under contract and so cannot work for him, otherwise we may be sued for obtaining money under false pretenses."

"Nonsense," said Karl. "Haven't we got degrees? Are we not geologists? Let us accept the offer. It will be easy to give him a geological survey of any part of Grand Fenwick he wishes. It will be just the same as that of the adjoining parts of France and Switzerland, and we can find that out from the university library before we leave."

Johannes shook his head. "Nothing in Grand Fenwick is like any other place in the world," he said. "I've a feeling this will hold true of its geology."

"My friend, licking stamps has cost you your courage," said Karl. "You must quit tomorrow while you still have a vestige of manhood left. We will go boldly to Grand Fenwick and give them a geological survey that will be remembered and indeed honored through the centuries for its high degree of imagination. I'll get it all together from the university library in advance. The whole survey will be ready, including maps of the various formations, before we even cross the borders of the Duchy. Leave it to me."

And so the two arrived in Grand Fenwick, took rooms at the Grey Goose and presented themselves to Mountjoy for their instructions.

The Count meanwhile had told both Bentner and Gloriana about Birelli's plan for the Grand Fenwick oil strike.

Bentner opposed it before Mountjoy had spoken more than a dozen words. "You're proposing an outright fraud," he said. "You are going to have Grand Fenwick exposed before the whole world as a nation of tricksters. When the truth is known—and it soon would be known—we will be the laughing stock of the whole world. The effect on our sales of wine and wool will be disastrous."

"Of course it's a fraud," said Mountjoy. "But are you really of the impression, after all your years of experience in government, that fraud, pretense, deceit and chicanery of every kind are not the legitimate and proper tools of statesmanship? Do you really believe that at international conferences, for instance, each nation honestly and frankly exposes its true position, announces its weaknesses, admits its inferiority, economically, militarily and at every level and out of it comes an equitable agreement?

"Of course not. If that were the case there would be no need for vigorous international espionage, for what are called 'intelligence officers' and 'political officers' attached to embassies in every country—each with his network of spies spread throughout the host nation. Espionage, deceit, fraud, the delicate coloring of the truth—these form the basis of international exchange and international concord. These are the things each nation expects of the other, and indeed were one to tell the truth, the whole truth and nothing but the truth, the delicate system would be destroyed. It is close to dishonorable, my friend, to be

115

truthful in dealings with other nations. Plain honesty is tantamount to betraying one's own country, and taking unscrupulous advantage of other nations—it is something so outrageous that it would not be tolerated in a civilized society." This left Bentner somewhat bewildered. But he still thought Mountjoy's plan too dangerous and said so.

"It can't work," he insisted. "You'd have to have oil wells pumping oil, not just a lot of derricks all over the place pumping nothing. There would have to be storage tanks full of oil and pipelines and how are you going to get away with that?"

"Mere details," said Mountjoy. "Leave all to me. If anything goes wrong I shall take complete responsibility and resign. Indeed retire from political life. You will then become Prime Minister with no rival in sight anywhere to challenge your position."

"You would stake your political career on this—this hoax?" asked Bentner incredulously.

"I would indeed," replied Mountjoy. "It is a small stake when so large a gain for mankind may be won."

Bentner went away disturbed, dissatisfied but sworn to secrecy. "I wash my hands of the whole thing," he said.

"In your case, that is the very best thing to do," said Mountjoy.

Gloriana was quite as dubious about the scheme as Bentner, though Mountjoy explained again and again the huge advantage which could be gained by stabilizing and reducing oil prices, revitalizing industry and checking a ruinous, international inflation.

"Even if those advantages are to be had," the Duchess said, "I don't see how you can pull the wool over people's eyes. I mean, we'll have to show some oil coming out of Grand Fenwick. Where would you put the two billion barrels of oil that Birelli is talking about?"

"Your Grace," said Mountjoy. "It would be better if you did not know at present. Should anything go wrong, I would not like the slightest tarnish of suspicion to touch you. I have told you of the matter out of a sense of personal loyalty. In fact it was my duty to inform you of it. Officially, Your Grace, I trust you will agree that I have told you nothing."

"Sometimes it is very hard to follow you, Bobo," said Gloriana.

"Your Grace," said Mountjoy, "you have unerringly hit upon the right position for you. You have had a chat with an old friend, Bobo. Your Prime Minister has told you nothing."

"I still don't know where you are going to put two billion barrels of oil," said Gloriana.

"I beg Your Grace to trust me when I assure you that I will find a container," said Mountjoy. After this interview he rang for his butler and said, "Have young Fotheringham, the steward, consult with whomever he needs to consult with and tell me what is the cubic capacity of the main dungeon."

"Cubic capacity, my lord?" said Meadows.

"Exactly. I would like to know how much water it would hold if it were made watertight."

The butler went off on his errand wondering whether his master was not slipping into senility at last, as some who opposed him believed. "Water in the dungeon," he muttered to himself. "I suppose he's not thinking of heating it for one last glorious hot bath?"

It was then that Johannes and Karl arrived and, having sent their names up to the castle, were granted an interview with Mountjoy.

"I'm delighted to meet you, gentlemen," said the Count. "I have an extremely important task for the two of you to perform and I may say I selected you for this task after examining the geological ability not only of all the graduates at Lausanne for the last five years but at Geneva as well.

"Among all those graduates, you two alone had all the qualifications required for the undertaking which I propose to put into your hands." They were sitting nervously in easy chairs on either side of the fireplace as Mountjoy spoke.

"We have?" Karl asked, surprised to find that his voice had risen an octave.

"You have indeed," said Mountjoy. "You are easily the worst geologists in Switzerland. Yet you have degrees in geology. That is exactly what I required."

Johannes was a little angry. "I protest, sir," he said. "I received my degree honorably from the University of Lausanne having passed the written requirements."

"Of course you did," Mountjoy said. "I have a copy of your thesis. It is one of many put on sale by an American publishing company to aid students facing the difficulty of passing an examination on a subject of which they know nothing. Astute people, the Americans.

"But, gentlemen, do not be disturbed about this. When you have been in the political field as long as I you will find it is quite normal, indeed a feature of our governmental system, to put into high office people who have not the slightest qualifications for the position. Film actors may these days become Presidents, and Presidents of dubious literary qualification, authors of best-selling books. In your own instance, being utterly unqualified for the work I wish you to perform is precisely what is required of you. I am delighted to have found you and delighted that you have agreed to accept my assignment."

"Your assignment, as I understand it, is to make a geological survey of a particular area of Grand Fenwick," Karl said.

"Correct—except for one provision, and before I reveal it to you I must bind you to complete secrecy. Not a word of what passes between us must ever get out of this study. Are we agreed?"

"Agreed," said Karl.

"Agreed," said Johannes. "But what is this provision?"

"I want you to find oil—oil in prodigious quantities," Mountjoy said. "Twenty billion barrels of highest-grade crude," he added.

Johannes and Karl both blanched, exchanged desperate looks and shook their heads.

"Out of the question," said Johannes. "Even though we are the worst geologists in Switzerland and perhaps in Europe, we do know that no oil is to be found in a granitic formation which constitutes the basic rock of Grand Fenwick. We looked that up in the library before we got here," he added.

"Gold?" suggested Karl. "I think you sometimes find gold in granite."

"How about tin?" asked Johannes.

"Oil," said Mountjoy firmly. "Twenty billion barrels of the finest oil. All you have to do is pick some suitable spot in the area called Perne's Folly, announce that examination of the rock formation indicates that a vast reservoir of oil lies below the surface, and have a test well drilled there."

"It'll be a dry hole," said Karl. "There won't be any oil."

"Come, gentlemen," said Mountjoy. "Despite your qualifications you should have a little more faith in yourselves. You can surely find some marine formation overlaid by a granite crust. Heavens, I could do that myself with a pickax and two buckets of shells brought from the nearest beach. Have you brought any electronic instruments—things for detecting what lies under the earth? I'd like to have something to impress people."

"We brought hammers," said Karl. "You know. For chipping pieces off rocks."

"Hmmm," Mountjoy said, disappointed. "All right. Do the best you can. Just a minute. I've remembered something."

He rang for the butler and when he appeared said, "My father had a pair of monstrous earphones here at one time when he was experimenting with an early wireless set. Something to do with crystals, if I remember correctly."

"Oh, yes," said the butler. "The whole apparatus is in the museum. I do believe it still works."

"Excellent," Mountjoy said. "Be good enough to bring it and give it to these gentlemen. They're interested in these things." The early-day crystal set with its two great earphones was produced and presented to the two neo-geologists. "I suggest one of you carry the box and the other of you put the earphones on and just plow around looking serious. If a man called Stedforth comes to question you, tell him you're geologists and you're making a survey of Perne's Folly at my request. He's the editor of our newspaper. Don't tell him you're looking for oil. If he wants to know anything more, send him to me. I'll deal with him."

"Won't he recognize the crystal set for what it is?" asked Johannes.

"Heavens no," said Mountjoy. "He's much too young. Just tell him it's a metal detector or a box of sandwiches. He really won't know the difference."

Somewhat dubiously the two returned to the tavern, determined to start their work on the following morning and get out of Grand Fenwick as fast as they could.

CHAPTER

13

Despite their good intentions, Johannes and Karl did not get to work early the following morning. After leaving Mountjoy the two stopped in at the public bar of the Grey Goose for a glass of October ale. This proved so good that they had one or two more, and under the friendly questioning of the people of Grand Fenwick who themselves dropped by for refreshment, confessed that they were geologists of some importance, had arrived from Switzerland, and were to undertake a survey in Perne's Folly.

Geologists were not unknown to Grand Fenwick. A thin stratum of pre-Cambrian formation, overlaid by granite, had been uncovered in cutting the two-lane road (it could hardly be called a highway) which circled the Duchy and eventually connected, outside the Duchy's border, with the French military road along which all commerce and mail for the Duchy traveled.

Pre-Cambrian deposits being rare in Europe, professors of geology often brought groups of students to examine the Grand Fenwick formation—a matter of the greatest pride to the people of the Duchy, who were delighted to know that their country, geologically at least, was a great deal older than much of the rest of the continent.

But that two geologists would want to investigate Perne's Folly set the Duchy tingling with excitement. It had been believed for centuries that there was treasure of some sort hidden there—gold, perhaps, or diamonds or, some said, rubies as big as pigeons' eggs lying in a cluster below the center of the stony valley. Otherwise why would that Frenchman Perne have bought the place in the first instance, centuries ago? Frenchmen were not fools when it came to money. That was something everybody knew. So when, after lying somewhat longer abed in the morning than they had intended, the two geologists arose to have breakfast, they found a score of Grand Fenwickians outside the inn, waiting to accompany them to the legendary but neglected valley.

Among them was Stedforth, editor of the Grand Fenwick *Times.*

To his questions they replied that they had been engaged to make a geological survey of the valley. They were not looking for anything in particular. They referred him to the Count of Mountjoy for further information. Stedforth knew of the visit of Birelli, had discovered that Birelli was a power in the world of oil, and now was confronted with two strange geologists making a survey of a little-known part of the Duchy.

He went immediately to Mountjoy and when he had

been admitted said in his somewhat abrupt manner, "One question. There are two geologists here in Grand Fenwick. Birelli was here a couple of weeks ago. Would I be very far wrong if I said that they were looking for oil?"

This was precisely the question that Mountjoy wanted to be asked. But he did not want it to appear that this was so. So he took his time answering, going to the lancet window which offered him his favorite view, and looking down into the courtyard where the white cross on the ground marked the landing spot for the helicopter. It had taken off with Birelli and would return in a few days with the scaffolding, draw works and other paraphernalia of a light drilling rig. So he gazed out of the window, seemingly in deep thought, and then turned slowly to face the expectant Stedforth.

"You can certainly say that the geologists are looking for oil," he said. "And I can give you some hint of the nature of Birelli's visit. As you know, the oil supply from the nations of the Persian Gulf has become both limited and expensive. It has also become uncertain due to the military situation. As I am sure you also know, there is a world search for a new source of oil. It appears that there is a prospect—let me emphasize the word 'prospect'—of there being oil in Grand Fenwick. In fairly large quantities," he added.

"More likely horsefeathers," said Stedforth. "Tell me— does this very unlikely prospect of yours result from a fresh study of previous geological surveys?"

"No," said Mountjoy. "It appears that satellites are capable of locating minerals, water and even oil reservoirs on earth, though by means I am quite unable to explain to you. A satellite photograph which has been lying around for several years awaiting examination indicated the presence of oil in Grand Fenwick—around the Perne's Folly area."

Stedforth was somewhat shaken by this unlikely news, but surprising things, he knew, were revealed by satellite photography of the earth so he withheld judgment.

That Mountjoy was lying did not trouble him a whit. But it was important to have a bolt-hole so that it could not be shown that he was lying.

"I'll admit that there is some hint that what appears to be a reservoir of oil in Grand Fenwick may instead be some deficiency in the emulsion on the negative," he said.

"If we did find oil in Grand Fenwick," said Stedforth, "where would we store it?"

This was another question that Mountjoy was very glad was being put to him.

"I'm certainly not going to put the Duchy to the expense of building a lot of storage tanks," he said. "We have one ancient reservoir which will make the building of storage tanks quite unnecessary for a long time."

"We have?" said Stedforth. "Where?"

"In the dungeon of the castle," said the Count. "I discover that it is entirely watertight, has remained so through the centuries. It will readily hold oil as well as water."

"How much oil?" asked Stedforth.

"Seven hundred thousand and twenty-four barrels," said Mountjoy. "That would do, I fancy, for the time being. If oil is discovered—'struck' I think is the proper term—we will merely have to construct a pipeline and pumps to get it from the well or wells to the castle dungeon for temporary storage."

"What about the Q-bomb?" asked Stedforth. "That's being kept in the dungeon for safety."

"It will be removed to somewhere equally safe, some-place where perhaps it will be of more service to mankind."

"Where?" demanded Stedforth. And Mountjoy, thinking back to happier times in the world—or so they seemed from this distance—recalled the famous reply of a famous American President and said, "Shangri-La."

Meanwhile, Johannes and Karl, wishing they hadn't drunk quite so much October ale, were stumbling about among the rocks in Perne's Folly watched by twenty or thirty people of Grand Fenwick who had nothing better to do. After consulting among themselves, these suggested to the two Swiss that they start at the north end of the valley where there was a large hill of stones under which all were convinced the treasure must lie. Despite their poor showing in geology, the two of them took one look at the hill and recognized it as a moraine—debris left by an Ice Age glacier. Still they walked around and over it, Karl wearing the earphones and Johannes carrying the crystal set and mysteriously manipulating the buttons which operated its primitive works.

Suddenly Karl stopped in the middle of the moraine.

"What is it?" Johannes demanded.

"This thing's working," Karl said. "I just heard part of a broadcast in French."

"What were they saying?"

"Hush. Give me that box." He took it from Johannes and began turning the buttons slowly. Very faintly he heard a voice saying, *"Ici Radio-Paris. Nous avons reçu de joyeuses nouvelles pour tout le monde. C'est qu'on a découvert une véritable mer de pétrole à Grand Fenwick. Le problème qui éxiste maintenant est: Où est Grand Fenwick?"*

"What are they saying?" Johannes demanded.

Karl looked around to see that no one of Grand Fenwick was within earshot.

"They're saying that a sea of oil has been found in Grand Fenwick," he said. "*Merde*. All we've been doing is walking around with this stupid thing. I haven't even looked at a rock yet."

"That's Mountjoy's work. He's forcing our hand," Johannes said. "He's making it so that we have to announce an oil strike here. Otherwise we forfeit our reputations."

"Forfeit our reputations?" Karl cried. "You out of your mind? What you mean is we'll preserve our reputations, as the two worst geologists in Switzerland. Still, I don't like being pushed around. Sounds like that Mountjoy doesn't trust us, announcing the news of an oil strike before we've announced it ourselves."

"Oh, I don't know," said the other reflectively. "Makes it easier. I mean, without a radio broadcast from Paris about the strike, who would believe us anyway?"

They came down from the top of the moraine and announced to those around that their instrument, though extremely sensitive, showed no indication of any treasure under the heap of stones left by the glacier. This discouraged the spectators, and it being now 11:30 A.M., which meant that the public bar of the Grey Goose would be open in half an hour, they trickled off in twos and threes, leaving Karl and Johannes alone.

They had brought some lunch with them, and sat down with their backs to a large worn boulder to eat. Before them, making a low table on which to put their sandwiches and Thermoses of tea, was another worn rock of a lightish color, from which the sun struck little sparkles of fire. Karl, pouring tea into his cup, upset some of it on the rock and moodily watched it soak into the surface.

"What do you remember about oil?" he asked his companion after a while.

"Oh. There were big forests and insects ate into the trees and killed them. So the trees fell down and got buried in the swampy ground out of which they grew and—"

"That's coal," Karl said. "Oil was different."

Johannes thought about it for a moment.

"I think it was dinosaurs," he said. "You know. Those big lizards. They died and got buried and turned to jelly and then to oil, and where a lot of them died, that's an oilfield. I read of it in an oil company advertisement in an American magazine. Why?"

"I think it's got something to do with the sea," said Karl. "Something to do with eensy weensy seashells or creatures which were just blobs of jelly like tapioca. I can't remember the name though. Miniformina or forminifera or something. Anyway, after billions of years they turned to oil. What I mean is that oil started in the bottom of the sea."

"Which is a long way from here," said Johannes taking a big bite of his sandwich and looking around at the valley of rocks strewn with Ice Age debris and oven-hot in the blinding sunlight.

"Is, but wasn't always," Karl said. "See that?" and he pointed to the dark spot on the rock where he had upset some tea.

"You spilled some tea," Johannes said. "So what?"

"Look a little closer," Karl said. "That rock's made up of tiny shells. There's masses of them all over it. They're not part of the glacier deposit. They were thrust up out of the bed of the ocean."

"Look," said Johannes. "We agreed in our second year at Lausanne that we weren't going to believe that crap, except for the purpose of passing exams. We agreed that the Bible was simple and probably right and everybody since Darwin has been wrong. Seashells come from the Flood."

"Okay," said Karl. "They come from the Flood. But they are seashells. And more than that, those eensy weensy seashells are the ones associated with oil deposits, I think. It's just possible that there is oil in Grand Fenwick."

"If there was the Americans or the British or the Arabs would have found it long ago," said Johannes.

"Nope. Because up to the present they weren't looking hard enough. What are you doing?"

"Shush," said Johannes. "I'm seeing if I can get more of that Paris broadcast." He held up a hand for quiet and with the earphones in place twiddled with the knobs of the crystal set. For a while he got only a series of whistles and howls which made him grimace and then a voice, a very faint voice saying ". . . *et pour bonbon nous avons pour vous ce canard délicieux—on met en évidence incontestable qu'on a découvert un mer véritable du pétrole en Grand Fenwick. La difficulté qui éxiste maintenant est de découvrir Grand Fenwick.*"

Johannes switched off the set and looked thoughtfully at his fellow geologist.

"They're making fun of us," he said. "They're broadcasting that the joke of the week is that an oil strike has been made in Grand Fenwick. We're the fall guys. We're the ones everybody will be laughing at when we announce that there is oil in Grand Fenwick as Mountjoy is paying us to do. Johannes Dupin and Karl Stampfli, the geological idiots of Europe."

"Well, wasn't that why we got the job in the first place?"

"The point is," said Johannes, "that we just may be able to turn the tables on them. We just may be able to find oil in Grand Fenwick. Then we'd have the last laugh. Let's look for more of these rocks with the eensy weensy shells in them."

"I've run out of tea," Karl said.

"You don't need tea. Just look closely at the rocks. The tea just makes it easier to find them." They spent the rest of the day searching the valley and found a number of shell-bearing rocks forming a rough dome to one side of the valley, which encouraged Karl. Domes, he said, were significant, but he couldn't remember whether in connection with salt or with oil deposits. "We'll look silly if we hit hot salt water," said Johannes, overcome by gloomy afterthoughts.

"We can't look silly whatever happens," replied his companion. "If we find oil we're brilliant. If we don't we announce that we have found it and Mountjoy has to supply the stuff and make the announcement good."

When they returned to the Grey Goose that evening they were tired but cheerful. The temptation to have a bottle of October ale was all but overwhelming, but Karl ordered the *vin du pays*—the great wine of the country known as Pinot Grand Fenwick.

"Nineteen sixty-five, gentlemen," said the bartender, pouring the wine as solemnly as if this were the world's first baptism. "What a year, premier grand cru. I assure you that I have put one bottle aside to be brought to me in my dying moments so I may leave the world joyfully and after my last sip leap straight into the arms of God."

They both sniffed and then sipped the wine and nodded in appreciation, for little as they knew of geology, they were Europeans and knew a great deal about wine.

"You are celebrating something, gentlemen?" asked the bartender.

"Yes indeed," said Johannes. "We celebrate the riches of the earth of Grand Fenwick."

Every ear in the bar was cocked to hear what would come next.

"Our wine, perhaps?" suggested the bartender.

"No," said Karl, who had finished his glass, rather loutishly in a couple of swallows and on whom the vintage was beginning to tell. "Not wine, gentlemen. Black gold. I say no more."

The two left while the bar buzzed with excitement over the discovery of black gold, whatever that might be, in Perne's Folly, rich with its legends of buried treasure.

CHAPTER

14

The next few weeks saw the importation into Grand Fenwick from France of a light drilling rig: draw works, pipelines and rotary pumps, and the plates out of which a small oil storage tank could be constructed. All this was arranged by Birelli, and the excitement was so great in the Duchy that work almost came to a standstill. Everybody now knew that the "black gold" which the two Swiss geologists had mentioned in the bar of the Grey Goose meant oil, and Mountjoy had called another special session of the House of Freemen to announce that his geological survey had resulted in a report that there was the highest expectation of a large reservoir of oil of excellent quality being found in Grand Fenwick.

The Count was rather irritated at the time with Birelli. Birelli, testing public reaction, had leaked the story in France previous to Mountjoy's announcement, resulting in the scoffing report on French radio already referred to. Birelli hadn't expected such a reaction, but then he was unaware of the centuries-old rivalry between France and Grand Fenwick. His serious mention at a reception given in his honor at the American Embassy in Paris of the prospect of there being oil in Grand Fenwick, exaggerated to an actual oil strike by reporters, had been taken as the richest joke of the year, particularly since it came from such an authority as himself.

As soon as the joke was out, world oil prices began to rise again, for the secret meaning of what Birelli had said was taken to be that there was not the slightest likelihood of any new oil strike being made anywhere on earth. The world, in short, had all the oil it was likely to get. Such a conviction could only lead to the hoarding of supplies and reduced distribution, forcing prices up higher, to Birelli's annoyance.

Mountjoy, however, went ahead with his end of the scheme. He had passed around a handful of the minute seashells which had been discovered by Johannes and Karl in Perne's Folly, and they had been examined with grunts and dubious looks by the members of the House of Freemen. They didn't look much like oil to anybody, but Bentner, who was of course in collusion with the Count, talked learnedly of oil shell and oil shale, mixing the two together, and Karl and Johannes being produced and asked to address the House acquitted themselves so well, and were so serious about the prospect of an oil strike, that Mountjoy concluded that not only had he hired the two worst geologists in Switzerland, but he had as a bonus received the two best actors in that nation.

The drilling platform was assembled on a place selected by the two geologists which was first cleared of boulders, and then the exploration rig was erected. Drilling did not commence until two pipelines had been laid underground—one from the French road outside the borders of the Duchy and the other to the dungeon of the castle. Everybody now understood the use of the one leading to the dungeon—that was the place where the oil was to be stored. Some thought that the smell would be more than those living in the castle—including Her Grace and Mountjoy—could tolerate. Others thought it dangerous—that there might be a fire or an explosion which would blow the castle up. Mountjoy pooh-poohed such thinking. Safety precautions, which he did not detail, would be quite sufficient. And the dungeon had always smelled, so the smell of oil would come almost as a relief to the occupants.

The other pipeline, leading first to a small pump and storage tank on the borders of the Duchy and then beyond to the French military road, required explanation, which was soon provided. This was the pipeline by which Grand Fenwick's oil would be conveyed out of the Duchy to be pumped into the big tank trucks which would soon be coming to collect it.

The opposite, of course, would be the case. The big tank trucks under the Birelli-Mountjoy agreement, would actually be pumping oil—millions of gallons of it—into the dungeon, whence, of course, it would later be pumped out, having in the interim become not Arabian but Grand Fenwick oil.

While all this business was going on—the erection of the drilling rig, storage tank, pipelines, Mountjoy had been writing to the sheiks of Saudi Arabia, Oman, Iraq and other Persian Gulf oil-producing nations, saying that he had a matter of high diplomatic importance to discuss with them, involving their security in the atomic age, and asking that a representative be sent to Grand Fenwick to open talks.

He had a plan of his own concerning the Q-bomb which he had not mentioned to Birelli, a plan which went beyond the stabilizing of international oil prices at some sensible figure, and ensuring continued supplies. He decided he must now discuss this plan with Her Grace and Bentner—with the latter with some reluctance, for Bentner, though the leader of the Duchy's Labor Party, was conservative to the core and abhorred any proposal which involved even the slightest degree of risk.

Mountjoy brought the matter up when the three of them were discussing the drilling preparations and the oil-strike scheme, Bentner dubiously, Gloriana with anxiety and Mountjoy with aplomb.

"Drilling will start in a week," he said. "We must expect a fortnight or so of drilling operations before we can announce that we have struck oil. There's some kind of heavy mud that has to be poured down an oil well when oil is discovered and we've had to order a few tons of that just to save face. My understanding is that it counteracts the pressure with which oil naturally gushes out of the ground and gives the driller and his crew time to get the Christmas tree in place."

"Christmas tree," exclaimed Gloriana.

"It's not a real Christmas tree," Mountjoy said. "It's a name given by drillers to an arrangement of pipes and valves by which they control the oil when it comes out of the ground. The first control, as I understand it, is obtained by the heavy mud of which I spoke. This is only a stopgap proceeding employed while this arrangement of pipes and valves and bypasses called a Christmas tree is put in place."

"But what we'll really have is a well full of some kind of heavy mud—right?" asked Bentner.

"Correct," said Mountjoy.

"I'm asking because those two Swiss whom I had for dinner the other night seem to think otherwise," said Bentner.

"I'm glad to hear that," said Mountjoy. "It confirms that they are indeed the two worst geologists in Switzerland. But I would like to inform Your Grace right now, and you too, my dear Bentner, of another scheme which I have felt it necessary to put in hand and to which I trust you will have no objection.

"While I was having my initial discussions with Birelli he made the elementary point that the Soviet Union is seeking to take possession of the oil-producing Persian Gulf nations by pressure from the outside and by subversion from within which would overthrow the present sheikdoms.

"I'm afraid he rather bored me with this particular analysis, for it has been the policy of Russia, whether under the Tsars or under its present regime, to dominate the Persian Gulf nations for the past two hundred years. But he went on to make the further point that no nation dare go to war over possession of the oil-producing nations of the Near East, for to do so would be to destroy the oil supplies which make them valuable to the world. This is childish thinking."

"Makes plain sense to me," said Bentner. "Without the oil those Arab countries are no use to anybody but camels."

"It makes plain sense to you because you do not realize how heavily the Western world depends on Persian Gulf oil, and by comparison, how little those supplies matter to Russia and her satellites, who get all the oil they need from their internal supplies. The West dare not go to war to secure the Near East OPEC nations. The Soviet Union, on the other hand, would gain, not lose, by such a war. Supplies for the Western world would be wiped out for perhaps ten or fifteen years, wrecking their whole economy. The supplies of the Soviet Union would scarcely be touched. Certainly their economy would scarcely be upset. The collapse of Western capitalism is the avowed aim of the Soviet. That aim would be moved very closer to achievement by a war cutting off the Persian Gulf oil flow."

"Wouldn't the Western world oil supplies be destroyed for all time?" asked Gloriana.

"No, Your Grace. The heaviest bombing will not destroy the underground reservoirs, only the refineries, storage tanks, wells and pipelines. You are too young to recall the heavy Allied bombing of the Romanian oilfields in the Second World War—oilfields which are now in full production and supplying the Soviet Union."

"Still don't see where we come in in all this," Bentner said.

"We perform one simple act," Mountjoy explained. "We make the Arabian states safe against attack by supplying them with a nuclear deterrent—the Q-bomb."

"Brilliant," said Bentner, who hated the Q-bomb. "I'll be glad to get rid of that thing."

"Heavens," Gloriana cried, dismayed. "It's terribly potent. Are you sure you can trust the Arabs with it?"

"It can destroy Europe and Russia too," said Mountjoy

calmly. "Yes. I am sure we can. The Arabs need it, in view of the Soviet threat, far more than we. The only trouble is that I can't get any of them to take it—or rather to send representatives here for a discussion about it. I've written to half a dozen Arabian nations, including Muscat, indicating strongly what I have in mind, and I haven't received a single reply. I may have to go to the Arabian peninsula myself. To Kuwait, perhaps, or Iraq, though I would prefer to deal with Saudi Arabia as being the most powerful."

Gloriana frowned. This was a terrible responsibility.

"Bobo, we're supposed to guard the bomb for others," she said.

"Your Grace, I have given this long and deep thought," said Mountjoy. "The original need for our guardianship—to establish nuclear peace among the nations—has now largely been met. Nuclear peace has been established by the appalling destructive power of the weapons which both sides possess. I might add that the proliferation of nuclear power stations, in my view, is also in itself a safeguard against war. Those nations possessing such stations, alarmed as they have been over the malfunction of one small valve, are surely not going to risk the hazard to their population of those power stations being bombed. No, the proper use of the Q-bomb now is to protect Western oil supplies. In the hands of the Saudi Arabians it will act as a powerful deterrent against the invasion of that country and its OPEC neighbors by the Soviet Union; they will never be invaded or bombed by the United States. But how to get the Arabian States even to reply to my letters—that is the real problem."

"I think I can help," Gloriana said.

"You can?" Mountjoy cried, surprised.

"Yes. Remember when Mr. Birelli was here and you sent me to Nice?"

"I do."

"I didn't go," Gloriana said. "I went to Paris instead. Nice is full of stuffy people at this time of the year and there is nothing to do there. In Paris I met a very nice man—at a discothèque."

"At a discothèque?" Mountjoy cried. "Surely Your Grace did not go to one of those places!"

"Yes I did," Gloriana said. "It was lots of fun. I haven't had any fun really since Tully died."

"You danced?" Mountjoy asked. His view of discothèque dancing came close to orgiastic ritual.

"Oh, Bobo," said Gloriana. "Of course I danced. It was fun. And I met this very nice man. He gave me his card." She opened her handbag and fumbled in it and took out an oblong of chaste pasteboard which she handed to Mountjoy.

Mountjoy fixed his monocle firmly in his eye, as if this would somehow absolve the card of whatever improprieties it represented, and stared at it for several seconds.

" 'Sheik Ali Muhmad Ibn Saud,' " he read aloud and then, dropping the card on his lap, he stared at Gloriana in surprise.

"You met Sheik Ali Muhmad Ibn Saud?" he asked. "In a discothèque? In Paris?"

"Yes," said Gloriana. "He danced very well—and he was educated at Eton. He was also an Oxford blue."

"Eton? Oxford?" echoed Mountjoy. And then, not quite as hopefully, "Discothèque?"

"Oh, Bobo," Gloriana said. "Dancing didn't end with the fox-trot and the Viennese waltz. It developed. It isn't so much a social thing now. It's a fun thing."

"So was the Viennese waltz, for those who knew how to get the most out of it," Mountjoy said. "Tell me, Your Grace, did the Sheik know who you were?"

"Of course," Gloriana said. "He has six wives, you know. It isn't his fault. It's his duty to his people. He has to have lots of children."

"Yes," said Mountjoy meditatively. "I remember his grandfather. I think he had a score of wives and sixty or seventy children. A highly patriotic man. Of course, one has to say this for it, that the grandfather's multiple marriages produced stability in a state which had been previously a hotbed of intertribal warfare. He did not er . . . make any suggestions regarding yourself?"

"He said he would like to add me to his list of wives, but he did not expect me to accept. He was very polite about it. He saw me back to my hotel and said that if at any time I was in need of help, I had only to contact him."

"Hmmm," said Mountjoy and looked somewhat more attentively at Gloriana. She was still a young woman, hardly more than in her middle forties. A mere child in fact. She had an excellent figure and an open, smiling, mischievous face. She rose and walked to a bureau containing a bowl of her favorite fruit, pomegranates, and Mountjoy, seeing the grace of her movement, the flowing lines of her figure, the elegance with which she stepped, raised his hand to the corner of his mouth and curled for a moment an imaginary mustache. Bentner glanced at him and nodded his head slightly.

"Your Grace," said Mountjoy when Gloriana returned with her pomegranate, "I think it might be in the interests of the world if you got in touch with this young man and asked him to pay an unofficial visit to Grand

Fenwick. I shall see that he is suitably accommodated in the castle and closely watched. You need have no fear."

"Oh, Bobo," said Gloriana. "You're such an old-fashioned darling." And she kissed him on the top of his head.

CHAPTER

15

Sheik Ali Muhmad Ibn Saud arrived in Grand Fenwick
a week later and charmed everybody. He was a slimly
built man in his mid-forties, of medium height, with a
nose like a hawk and eyes which changed from soft devo-
tion to sword-bright anger in a moment. He moved with
the grace of a cat and he had about him at all times three
enormous Arabs in flowing robes, impassive as statues and
capable, it seemed, of mayhem or murder without the
slightest show of emotion.

Gloriana called them the Three Terrors.

But the Sheik attracted everybody by his personality.
He was deeply read in Western literature, knowledgeable
on Western art and yet had a light sense of humor which
made him the most agreeable of companions.

Mountjoy had hoped to start serious talks with the Sheik
the day after his arrival. But instead he got the same treat-
ment which he himself had devised for Birelli. The Sheik

managed to keep him at a polite, good-humored distance and spent the greater part of his time with Gloriana. This made Mountjoy very nervous and Bentner too, for they had known Gloriana since she was a child and felt protective toward her. Polished sophisticate that he was, Mountjoy began to exhibit all the symptoms of a suburban father whose daughter is constantly out late—and Gloriana was constantly out late.

The Sheik had no need to be concerned about money, and had arrived in France in his own plane, a DC-10 equipped like a hotel, and in Grand Fenwick in his $100,000 custom-built Maserati which had been sent ahead to await him and now gleamed in the straw of a disused stable. He took Gloriana for a three-day cruise on his yacht in the Mediterranean, driving to Cannes. Although Mountjoy was also invited, he got terribly seasick and was hardly in touch with what was going on. On return to Grand Fenwick, Gloriana and her Sheik went to Paris for two days, and when they got back, Mountjoy took Gloriana aside and gave her a lecture on propriety.

"He's just great fun to be with," said the Duchess. "There's nothing more to it than that. I'm quite safe. Remember he has six wives."

"That's exactly what I am remembering," said Mountjoy. "A man with one wife may become devoted to her. But a man with six wives is likely to become devoted merely to women in general. I'm sure I don't have to talk to Your Grace about the—"

"Really, Bobo," said Gloriana. "Remember I was married ten years. There isn't really much that you have to warn me about."

Mountjoy sighed. "You're a very beautiful woman, Your Grace," he said.

"Perhaps," said Gloriana. "Sometimes it's a nuisance being a Duchess. However, I do not forget that I am a Duchess and have a responsibility to my people which I must put before my personal wishes. Freddie is sympathetic. He has the same thing."

"Freddie?" said Mountjoy.

"That's what they called him at Eton. He prefers it to Ali Muhmad Ibn Saud. He's really very nice, Bobo. I wish you could get to know him better."

"So do I," Mountjoy said. "After all, I did invite him here so we could talk of matters of some importance."

"About the Q-bomb and this oil business," Gloriana said. "I don't think you'll have too much trouble. I've softened him up a bit. I think he'll take the Q-bomb. As a favor."

"As a favor?" cried Mountjoy. "I'm offering him nuclear parity with the Soviet Union and the United States and he thinks he's doing me a favor?"

"They don't think like we do," Gloriana said. "They think that being in possession of a huge percentage of the world's oil resources they already have the equivalent of the Q-bomb, though it is economic in nature. Also there's the problem that if any one Arab state has nuclear arms, the others might regard that as a threat to them. So it would have to be owned in common and that's difficult because some don't really trust the others."

"Eton," pondered Mountjoy, shaking his head. "I always held that Winchester was the better school in which to Anglicize foreign students."

"Of course, it would be different if I accepted Freddie's offer of marriage," Gloriana said. "I'd be his seventh official wife and he has a lot of concubines. But I would be

144

his chief wife—or at least that's what he says now. And I could live in Grand Fenwick, just occasionally visiting his kingdom. But as the chief wife and a ruler in my own right there would be a compact between Grand Fenwick and Saudi Arabia and the—"

"Outrageous," Mountjoy cried. "I cannot permit Your Grace to become a pawn in the power politics of the Near East, a chattel to be disposed of in marriage for the benefit of some Arabian despot."

Gloriana eyed him thoughtfully. Was it possible that he was beginning to slip? Was it possible that his keen, informed, subtle mind was being infected by senility of which the first symptoms were his worries over her relations with the Sheik and his seeming inability to anticipate the Arab point of view on nuclear armament?

But Mountjoy soon put those fears to rest.

"You might mention to . . . er, Freddie," he said, "that I have received a communication from Kuwait and Oman and Iraq each expressing an interest in sending a diplomatic mission to Grand Fenwick."

"Have you?" said Gloriana, very surprised.

"Yes," said Mountjoy smoothly. "From the Three Terrors in fact. Each separately and secretly. It appears that they serve more than one master." He gave a slight smile and added quietly, "Freddie, apparently without his knowledge, has brought his brother Arab states with him. But I'd like to deal with Freddie first." Gloriana was still staring at him in disbelief when he bowed and left.

An hour later Freddie the Sheik, as Mountjoy was beginning to think of him, sent a message by the bodyguard representing Kuwait asking whether he might have a formal interview with Mountjoy after dinner. Mountjoy replied that he would be honored to have the Sheik as his dinner guest and they could talk later. He had inquired of the kitchen staff and discovered that Freddie did not require a special menu, and they had an excellent meal together from which the Three Terrors were excluded. Freddie politely refused wine and contented himself with many cups of black coffee, sweet as molasses.

"I have been watching events in the Moslem and Arab nations for some fifty years," said Mountjoy suavely, "and they have arrived at the point which I expected: the Persian Gulf peoples, if you will excuse so generalized a phrase, are in peril of being seized by the Soviet and brought under their dominance. I expect, Your Excellency, that you have yourself foreseen this threat and laid plans to meet it. I would like to be of what service I can in discussing your plans and helping to further them."

"To have an offer of both counsel and aid from so distinguished a statesman as yourself is extremely gratifying," said Freddie. "May I ask in commencing that you review the situation as you see it and I can then, perhaps, add such details to complete the picture as may not have come to your notice."

Mountjoy reviewed the situation. The world supremacy of the OPEC nations, particularly those situated around the Persian Gulf, had made them a prime target for annexation by the Soviet Union. The anti-American moves in oil-rich Iran, and the Soviet adventure into Afghanistan, against which no countermove of strength had been made by the United States, undoubtedly encouraged the Soviet planners to believe that if they moved militarily into the Arabian nations, the American response might be equally ineffective.

Against an overt threat, the Arabian countries, however modern their armies, could not make effective resistance since they lacked nuclear power. It was not the actual use of nuclear power but the threat of its use which had preserved peace among the world's nations for so long.

In this situation, the real salvation of the Arab nations was to have nuclear potential of their own. Grand Fenwick could offer them that potential with the Q-bomb. It need never be used; in fact it must never be used. The fact that it was in the possession of the Arabian nations would be sufficient to protect them. It would make them independent of the patronage-profit of others. It would preserve their self-respect. As for internal dissension fomented against the present regimes, that would be a matter they could best handle themselves and one to which they were undoubtedly attending at the present time.

"We of Grand Fenwick take a great risk in making this offer," Mountjoy concluded. "I have no need to point out to you that if an internal revolution, instigated by the Soviet or any others, were successful, then the Q-bomb (which, I will add parenthetically, is still far more powerful than any fission or fusion weapon yet devised) would fall into the hands of the revolutionaries. However, we must be and are prepared to accept that risk."

When the Count had concluded, Freddie said, "You will allow me to point out that the Q-bomb, however potent it may be, is an outdated weapon in that it is only a bomb. It has to be dropped from an airplane—a ridiculously easy target these days—instead of being delivered by a supersonic intercontinental rocket."

"It doesn't have to be delivered at all," said Mountjoy smoothly. "All you have to do is explode it right where it lies. The effect would be to destroy on the instant most of Europe and Russia."

"Ourselves as well," said Freddie.

"It is a characteristic of atomic warfare that there are likely to be no survivors," said Mountjoy. "That is what makes the threat of atomic warfare so excellent a guarantor of peace."

"Shooting down an airplane carrying the Q-bomb would have the same effect?" Freddie asked.

"Precisely," said Mountjoy. "It's an unattackable weapon."

"And unusable," said Freddie.

"I wouldn't bet on that," the Count said. "Would you?"

"I don't know," Freddie responded.

There were a few moments of silence and then Freddie said, "You should know that our own analysis of Russian policy shows no indication that the Soviet Union has the slightest desire to acquire our oil wealth. They have oil supplies of their own. Their industry is not as extensive as that of the Western world. Their reliance on oil for energy is much less."

"May I remind you," said Mountjoy, "that the fundamental doctrine of the Marxists is that the collapse of the capitalist West will come about through economic disaster. The rule book says that every method must be used which will hasten that disaster. I can think of nothing so effective as the depriving of the West of the greater portion of the oil needed to run its industry and sustain its standard of living.

"In this sense, I regret to say, the American oil companies who have been buying their oil cheaply from you and selling it at a grossly inflated price have become the allies of the communists. Capitalism and communism have, alas, only tunnel vision." He thought for a moment of the lions and the unicorns on the ceiling of his bedroom painted by Derek of Pirenne in the fifteenth century.

"We unicorns," he said, "see further. Ours is a panoramic view."

"Unicorns?" echoed Freddie.

"Thinkers. Artists," said Mountjoy. "You are surely such and not merely a very wealthy young man with all the material delights of the world at his disposal."

"Why should you make that assumption?" asked Freddie.

"A matter of observation," replied the Count. "You own a Maserati. Nothing vulgar. And you have refrained from painting it a bright red."

Mountjoy rose slowly and walked to a humidor on his huge desk (for they were talking in his study) and selected a Corona panatela, which he first examined carefully to see by its color that it was mature, and then, having sniffed it delicately for further assurance, lit slowly with a large wooden match.

"It's curious," he said, "and sad that one lives too short a life for meditating on these things. But I find myself amused that I decided I could trust the Q-bomb to you and with it hundreds of millions of lives while I have been highly disturbed for some days about trusting you with Her Grace, Gloriana the Twelfth."

"Oh, you had reason to be disturbed," said Freddie coolly. "A man such as I has but one purpose for the greater number of women he meets. They are there to be enjoyed and then comes a parting, with gifts, of course, when they may find some other man. But I have found in your Duchess another quality. Something unique which should not be used nor hurt. She is a rider of the wind, and under the hand of Allah."

"A rider of the wind?" said Mountjoy. "I don't follow."

"'Those who move as swift as desert wind
Find all about them silent, calm and mild.
The unmoving mountains moan under its wrath.
The riders of the wind but hear and smile.'

"The translation is not good. But perhaps it will give you a sense of what I find in your graceful Duchess. I will dream of her often. I will not harm her."

Mountjoy watched a blue spiral of cigar smoke writhe upward from the end of his panatela and said, "Perhaps it is only in the West that chivalry is dead. Perhaps among your people, a touch yet remains. I salute you, sir."

He raised his glass and while sipping the wine wondered whether some centuries before an earlier Mountjoy, carrying the red cross of a crusader over his coat of mail, might not have in the same manner saluted some warrior of the great Suleiman. He thought it probable. Life was little if it had no continuance, generation to generation, no echo from one century to another.

"I shall send the Q-bomb to your country tomorrow," he said. And so it was agreed.

CHAPTER

16

The Q-bomb did not actually leave for Saudi Arabia until two weeks later, and then of course it left by the helicopter which Mountjoy had borrowed from Birelli and was able to pass through national frontiers without inspection as being an official aircraft on a diplomatic mission. Up to that point the helicopter had been used to fly in the oil-drilling equipment needed for the Grand Fenwick oil strike. It could not be spared earlier. When it was sent on its mission, the pilot did not know what he was flying and only Mountjoy, Bentner, Gloriana and Dr. Kokintz in all Grand Fenwick knew that the Q-bomb was about to leave the Duchy.

Kokintz had had to be brought in on the secret, for it was necessary that he first inspect the bomb and make it safe for transport. He spent two days working on it. He insisted on being alone, and packed the bomb, swaddled in the fleeces of Grand Fenwick, in a wine cask as a guarantee against its detonation by any vibration, however heavy, to which it might be subjected. He wrote out a long list of step-by-step instructions for removing the bomb from the cask so that it might be placed in an appropriate strongroom, under guard, when it arrived in Saudi Arabia.

Then the bomb was sent off to the relief of Bentner, though Gloriana had her misgivings.

"It's curious," she said. "But I've lived with it so long in the dungeon of the castle that, appalling as it is, I've come to think of it as part of Grand Fenwick. Maybe what I really think is that we are the only nation in the world that can be trusted with it." Kokintz, who had been busy in his laboratory for weeks now, and who had devised a novel kite for Katherine, was present when this statement was made.

"Do not worry, Your Grace," he said. "No harm will come to anybody. I am quite sure about that."

He had a kindly way of speaking and Gloriana found herself curiously reassured by what he said.

Drilling at Perne's Folly having proceeded now for several days with a high-speed rotary drill, equipped with a multiple-head diamond bit, the Grand Fenwick well had reached a depth of over six thousand feet and Mountjoy felt that it was getting to be time to announce that oil had been struck.

He therefore consulted with Birelli and they agreed on November 7 of that year for the delivery of the first tank trucks of oil (by night, of course) to Grand Fenwick. The oil would be pumped from the tank trucks through the short pipeline leading from the Grand Fenwick frontier to the well. From there it would go to a small storage tank erected nearby to give the appearance that it was oil from the well, and from the storage tank to the dungeon of Grand Fenwick castle, accompanied by the joyous news of an oil strike.

Two tank trucks of oil, it was thought, would be enough for the first delivery, for the business of pumping the heavy mud down the well as a piece of essential showmanship, together with the erection of the Christmas tree over the wellhead, had also to be attended to. Thereafter a fleet of tank trucks would be on hand, pumping oil into the dungeon while the pretense was maintained that the oil was coming from the dungeon, having originated in the well.

These details arranged, November 8 was agreed as the day when Mountjoy would announce to the House of Freemen that oil had been struck in the Duchy, that the reservoir of oil was enormous, amounting to twenty billion barrels at a conservative estimate, and that the oil would be sold to all desiring it at fifteen dollars a barrel, which was twenty dollars a barrel lower than the lowest price offered by any of the OPEC nations.

The two geologists, Karl and Johannes, had of course predicted time and again that oil would be struck. The French radio and media generally through Europe and even the United States regarded the whole thing as a hoax, particularly after having looked into the technical qualifications of Johannes and Karl. "Grand Fenwick oil strike" became a phrase in popular use to indicate something thought ludicrous. When for instance Soviet scientists announced that they had produced a hybrid of rye and Indian corn which increased egg production in the USSR by 80 percent, people just smiled and said, "Sure. And they've struck oil in Grand Fenwick." Similarly when the President of the United States announced that if re-elected he would cut taxes and at the same time balance the budget that was called a "Grand Fenwick oil strike."

The night preceding the day selected had been cloudy, and the evening air heavy with an unnatural, summerlike heat. People predicted that there would be a thunderstorm, and Ted Weathers, who had for years been complaining of pains in his head caused by radiation emitted by the Q-bomb, announced that these pains were now worse and there was going to be both a thunderstorm and a deluge of rain. He therefore spent an extra two hours in the bar of the Grey Goose and said that he remembered in his father's time there had been a like night and that it portended a big change in the Duchy's affairs.

"And what change came about then?" he was asked. He took a cautious sip of his wine and said, "Vine rot. There was only ten good barrels of Pinot produced in the whole country and I remember my dad saying that right here in this tavern they was selling Sauterne from France—aye, and beginning to like it. Surprising what people will get used to drinking when they has to," he added. "But mark my words. Something's in the air. Something is going to happen that will affect us all."

There were heavy thunderstorms that night, together with displays of lightning which threw the massy crag of Grand Fenwick Peak into brutal relief against the sky. For several hours the thunder rumbled about the mountains and then died away, and after deluges of rain, morning came quiet as a maiden and sweet with birdsong.

Mountjoy, breakfasting in his silken dressing gown as usual, told Meadows to lay out the dark formal suit from Tillot of Bond Street with the cutaway coat, which, though generations out of date, he wore for special sessions of the House of Freemen. He requested a small white rosebud for his buttonhole and brushed his silver hair with special care before the full-length oval tilting mirror, a gift to one of his ancestors from Metternich following the Congress of Vienna.

(The story is related in the history books of Grand Fenwick, and it is deserving of the credence given to the accounts in the histories of other nations, that when Napoleon tried to rally the remnants of the Guard at Waterloo for one great thrust on Wellington's center, they were met by a volley of arrows from the stout Grand Fenwick contingent, which threw the Guard into unprecedented confusion so that Blücher had time to arrive on the field and win the day.)

He breakfasted off the tray of Regency silver, his dress scrupulously attended to, his rosebud in place and the silver chain of his monocle looping gracefully from his waist pocket. Mountjoy then sent a message to Her Grace that he trusted he would have the pleasure of seeing her enter the chamber in half an hour. Gloriana, who had been awaiting the message, assured him that she would be there and got out of bed. She was a quick dresser, and was beautifully attired in twenty minutes and on her way, though conscious that her left shoe was a little loose and she should have stuffed some tissue paper in the toe.

The whole House arose when Her Grace entered and, bowing to both sides (Mountjoy's Conservatives and Bentner's Laborites), took her seat on the thronelike chair above and behind the Speaker, provided for her.

She was a bit nervous. She was about to hear, for the first time in her life, a big fat lie told to the parliament and people of Grand Fenwick by the government in the person of the Count of Mountjoy, whom she adored. She hoped that at the very last Mountjoy would repent and not go through with it. He'd given her examples, the evening before, of real whoppers told by people like Palmerston and Disraeli and even Gladstone whom everybody knew was the greatest statesman England ever had. But that didn't really comfort her. She didn't think of the British as foreigners, of course, but on the other hand they were not of Grand Fenwick. So it might be all right for them to lie and be devious, but it just wasn't right for Grand Fenwick, which she always felt represented no mighty and imperialistic power, but just the smaller people of the earth everywhere.

"If *they* find out we're lying," she said to Mountjoy, "they'll just have nobody to go to for the truth."

"It will not be Grand Fenwick that lies but I," replied Mountjoy, "and I will take the shame—if discovered. It is a poor man indeed who will not lie for his nation."

"I just think the whole thing isn't necessary," Gloriana replied.

The business of the day opened with the readings of some small bills with which members were fully acquainted, and for which they had already expressed their hates and loves. A bill to import Swedish larch for the improvement of the forest of Grand Fenwick. That was one of them. It was going to be voted down despite the support of arbiculturalists, because nobody wanted Swedish trees growing in the forest of Grand Fenwick. A bill to prohibit for all time the building of a nuclear power station in Grand Fenwick. That was another, and it was likely to be heavily amended before passage. The younger people were vigorously for it and had marched through the Duchy with signs proclaiming "No Nukes" and "Remember Three Mile Island," which puzzled those in the

Duchy who had never heard of Three Mile Island. In the same way they had marched during the Chavez attempt to organize the grape workers of California with signs shouting "Don't Buy Grapes" though 60 percent of the country's revenue derived from grapes.

The older voters wanted to amend the bill to limit its provisions to ten years, arguing that it was wrong to legislate with finality for the unborn of Grand Fenwick, which would make the dead the rulers of the living. So another bill was being prepared which limited the effectiveness of any statute to twenty years and that was likely to meet heavy opposition too. All these necessary but (in the circumstances, petty) proposals had to be dealt with even at this special session before, having caught the Speaker's eye, Mountjoy rose to make his announcement.

He first obtained complete silence and then examined the whole House, his face grave and determined. It seemed to Bentner as Mountjoy fingered his monocle, which he always put in his right eye when about to make an announcement of some importance, that his fingers trembled slightly.

Bentner's heart went out to him. They'd been political enemies for over a score of years. Bentner turned to his nearest companion and said, his eyes still on the Count, "Here it comes. Poor bastard."

"Your Grace, Mr. Speaker, honorable members of the House," said Mountjoy. "I have an announcement to make of the utmost importance to the people of the Duchy and indeed to the people of the Western world, as also to the people of those nations whom we have referred to in the past as the Middle East. It is an announcement perhaps not unexpected, and yet one which I trust will fill you both with pleasure and an increased sense of the responsibility of this Duchy to the world at large.

"You are all aware that following a geological survey made in the Duchy by two distinguished Swiss geologists, drilling operations were started just a few weeks ago in the area known to you as Perne's Folly.

"For the past week, due to certain indications reported by the drilling crew, the area of operations has been blocked off from public access. Drilling for oil is not without its dangers. However, I have been keeping in close touch with the drilling operations and have been sent daily samples of the cores obtained from the well. These cores, as you perhaps know, are samples of the strata being drilled through and are an indication of what is likely to be found in or beyond them.

"The House might like to hear details of these cores for the last few days." (Some members groaned. Mountjoy was more than usually wordy, they thought, and they didn't give a hang about the cores.)

"Several hundred feet of granite had first to be penetrated," Mountjoy continued, "when a stratum of limestone, which is of course of marine origin, was entered. Then came more granitic rock in what are called 'dikes,' that is, uppourings of magma from the center of the earth. Then some sandstone and in the last three days, the type of limestone, or marine formation, which indicated an ancient coral reef."

These details of coring had actually been supplied by Johannes and Karl to the Count, and he was surprised that two so deficient in geological knowledge still had sufficient imagination to come up with them. He presumed they had taken them from some successful well drilled elsewhere.

"This morning, at five-fifteen, when drilling operations were resumed after the storm, a large amount of gas started to emerge from the wellhead. It was controlled with the appropriate mud. The mud was then lightened when the gas pressure had been ascertained and brought under control. And I am delighted to inform you that oil of the highest quality has been struck, of which there are now several hundred gallons in storage in the dungeon of this castle."

He paused, and in a silence which could almost be heard, the members looked at each other, surprised, and then slowly back at the Count. Only Bentner looked at his hands, his ears beginning to grow red.

Mountjoy was unperturbed.

"The geological report is," he continued, "that this Duchy has beneath it a vast sea—I might say ocean—of oil. I do not pretend to understand the scientific means by which such an estimate can be made. They involve the use of complicated instruments based on some principle concerning sound waves with which I will not trouble members. But the estimate—a conservative one—is that the usable oil reservoir amounts to twenty billion barrels. Grand Fenwick, then, is in a position to take its place among the OPEC nations of the world as not so long ago we took our place among the atomic powers.

"If we call upon those virtues of prudence and wisdom which have served us so well in the past, I believe we can, with such reserves of oil at our disposal, bring back some sense not only to the world oil supply situation, but to the price at which that oil is supplied. We can, in short, avert the economic catastrophe which faces the Western world in its energy crisis."

He stopped speaking again and the same silence of incredulity and amazement seized the House. To be sure, Karl and Johannes had talked about the probability of striking oil in Perne's Folly and kept on talking. But so had French radio and the world media and such was the effect of this mocking propaganda that many in Grand Fenwick had come to regard the two geologists as enthusiastic cranks.

From the back of the House, by the heavy entrance doors of smoked oak, there now came the sound of scuffling. It was muffled at first, grew louder, a shout or two was heard and then, past the halberdiers guarding the doors, came Karl and Johannes. They burst right into the center of the chamber, stood stock-still for a moment, overcome by what they had done, and then turning to Mountjoy, whose look would have reduced them to ashes were that possible, Johannes shouted, his voice trembling with excitement:

"We've done it! We were right! We've struck oil!"

The Speaker banged with his gavel and ordered the two thrown out. The halberdiers came forward to evict them. They had Karl and Johannes by the arm and were about to effect their purpose when Mountjoy signaled them to desist.

"I ask the pardon of Your Grace, of you, Mr. Speaker, and of the honorable members of the House for this intrusion," he said. "These two young men, who were not on the drilling rig last night, have undoubtedly been overcome by the vindication of their views, so long mocked at by others, and of which they have just heard."

He turned to the two. "I have already informed the House that oil has been struck at Perne's Folly."

"But it *has* been—it really *has* been," said Karl. "It's

flowing right now at the rate of thirty barrels an hour."

"It's the biggest strike of the century," said Johannes.
"It's top-grade crude. And we are the two finest geologists
in Switzerland." And ignoring the House in all its dignity,
the pair started a jig together.

CHAPTER

17

Mountjoy had been known to panic—or at least come close to panic—on but one occasion in his life. That was when, with an important ceremony before him, he discovered that there was not a single pair of black silk socks in his wardrobe to go with his striped pants. He solved the situation by borrowing those of his butler.

He came equally close to panic now, but in the confusion of the geologists doing their jig on the floor of the House, with the Speaker banging with his gavel to restore order and the halberdiers finally removing the triumphant duo from the chamber, he had time to recover his nerve.

He knew he must give no indication whatever of being troubled, particularly since that idiot Bentner opposite him was close to a nervous breakdown and actually had a rather grubby handkerchief clasped over his face as if he were crying. He glanced at Gloriana and was relieved to see that she was smiling, as if she had forgotten that it was her birthday and someone had reminded her with a present of a delightful cake. Actually what made her so happy was that Mountjoy hadn't had to tell a whopper and the armor of her knight was unsullied.

Order was eventually restored, though for a moment or two there came through the corridors the cry of Johannes and Karl, "We were right. We are the most famous geologists in Switzerland." Mountjoy still had the floor and now, fully in control of himself, though the devils of disaster flashed here and there in the back of his mind, spoke as smoothly as ever before.

"Once again may I request of Your Grace, you, Mr. Speaker, and you also, honorable members, that you overlook this scene of unpremeditated jubilation. It is perhaps not without significance that our two geologists, brilliant as they are, come from the French-speaking part of Switzerland and may then lack a certain self-control. Also they are young, and the exuberance of youth must be given its place, even in the august chamber of this, one of the world's oldest parliaments.

"You have heard from me, then, that we are the national possessors of a vast reservoir of oil. I find it my duty to announce this officially to you even before there was time to put before you for your consideration any well-developed government plan for the sale and disposal of this precious commodity.

"Before the recent interruption, I did, however, express the hope that through the exercise of prudence and wisdom we may be able to bring some reason back into the price at which oil is sold and the quantity in which it is supplied. I would like to know whether it is the sentiment of the House that we seek no profit from this oil, but, regarding energy in the same way as we regard air—that is as a needed human resource—supply it to those requiring oil for the industrial health and progress of their nations, at a sum sufficient only to cover the costs of extraction, pumping and storage."

"Do you wish a vote taken upon this question?" the Speaker asked.

"An expression of sentiment—by voice," replied Mountjoy. "Not binding upon individuals but indicating their general wishes."

The vote was taken and the ayes were in the overwhelming majority. Indeed only Bentner voted no and that, as he explained later, was out of force of habit as Leader of the Opposition.

When this was done the Speaker adjourned the session, there being no more business to discuss, and Mountjoy took Bentner by the sleeve and asked him to meet immediately in the Count's study to discuss this catastrophic turn of events. He also asked Her Grace to join them and soon the three were seated before a nice wood fire, for the day had turned cold following the thunderstorms of the night before.

Mountjoy was himself again—not panicked, but exulting in the new problems and perhaps dangers which surrounded him. His ideas always flowed swiftly at such times and he gained a decisiveness which was (for him at least) exhilarating. Gloriana was happy. Bentner was muddled. He kept murmuring to himself and shaking his head and when Mountjoy, irritated, asked him to speak up and state plainly what was troubling him, Bentner, still muttering, raised his voice and demanded plaintively, "What are we going to do with all that oil?"

"Heavens," said Mountjoy, "if that is all that is bothering you, you may put your mind at rest immediately. I will obviously call Birelli and tell him to stop shipments. That will take care of a great deal of the problem. I fancy he'll be rather glad. Courageous man. He stood to lose billions in an audacious attempt to stabilize the world oil price. There is always, Your Grace, a high reward for courage, while the faint-hearted can expect nothing but disaster. You will pardon me?" He walked to his desk and picked up the old-fashioned telephone, jiggling the receiver. It was a minute or two before he got the girl on the exchange, who was knitting a pair of rompers for her younger sister's baby—due in three months. She didn't of course know whether to use blue or pink so she was using black.

"The stains won't show up so much," she explained practically.

"Mountjoy here," the Count said unnecessarily when he had at last gotten her attention. "I want you to get hold of Mr. Alfonso Birelli in Paris." He gave the number and added, "If he's not there ask Miss Thompson, his secretary, to find out where he is and have him call me immediately."

"Is she the one that was so friendly with Mr. Bentner?" said the exchange girl, whose name was Elise. "Never quite trusted her somehow. Too sweet. You know how it is."

"Yes," said Mountjoy heavily. "I know how it is. Please put my call through immediately. It is urgent."

"Haven't got a line open," said Elise.

"Well, sweep the board clean," cried the exasperated Count. "Disconnect everybody and connect me."

It took forty-five minutes to get the call through to Paris. There were several disconnects and Mountjoy found himself talking to an angry operator in Lyons from whom he could not get disentangled, for every time he picked up the telephone, there she was. Eventually the connection was made and he had Birelli on the line.

"Mountjoy here," he said. "I have wonderful news for you. We've struck oil, an estimated twenty billion barrels of it, here in Grand Fenwick."

"The tank trucks arrived on time, eh?" said Birelli smoothly. "Great. They'll come rolling in every night now until you're floating on a sea of oil down there."

"My dear Birelli," said Mountjoy. "That's what I am trying to tell you. We *are* floating on a sea of oil down here. We have struck oil in Grand Fenwick."

"As we agreed," said Birelli.

"No. Not as we agreed. It actually happened. Real oil coming out of the ground."

"You're crazy."

"My dear Birelli, that is not a phrase used among gentlemen. I am not crazy. We have struck oil—an ocean of it. I tire of the phrase. Here in Grand Fenwick. Please do not send any more. It's quite superfluous. Indeed embarrassing. There are only two automobiles here and a small power station and the thing for heating my bath. We just cannot absorb several hundreds of barrels a day."

"Look," said Birelli, in a kind of desperate and hoarse whisper as if he were having a heart attack. "Look. I've put every nickel of liquid cash I can find into the purchase of oil for this scheme. I've pledged the total assets and more of the vast conglomerate I control. I've blackmailed and bullied every banking institution in Europe and the United States into lending me the last penny they can come up with without going broke themselves.

"I've done it all to have enough oil at my disposal to

tumble the price per barrel ten or fifteen dollars by pretending it all comes from Grand Fenwick. And now you tell me you have oil in Grand Fenwick. Do you know what that means? It means that I'm ruined. So is my whole financial empire. This time next week, I'll be lucky if I can raise enough credit to buy a cup of this lousy French coffee. You've betrayed me, God dammit. Betrayed me."

"Sir," said the Count. "You forget yourself. Nobody has ever said he was betrayed by a Mountjoy. I have not betrayed you. I have followed our agreement to the comma. What we pretended to expect, but didn't actually expect, has happened. We have been unfortunate enough to discover an ocean of oil—oh, hang the phrase—here in Grand Fenwick which makes your purchases, as far as I can see, unnecessary."

"What am I supposed to do about it?" Birelli demanded.

Mountjoy, who had lit a panatela to soothe his nerves during the bout with the telephone operator at Lyons, exhaled a thin stream of aromatic smoke over the glowing tip of the cigar.

"Go ahead as planned," he said calmly.

"Go ahead as planned?" exploded Birelli. "Do you realize that I have invested or pledged sixty billion dollars —I will repeat that figure—sixty billion dollars in two billion barrels of oil—and it was all absolutely unnecessary?"

"My good Birelli," said Mountjoy. "This is no time for either of us to lose our nerve. It is no time for either of us to change horses since we are in midstream. I strongly suggest that you suspend your oil shipments in view of the enormous production of our one well in Grand Fenwick. But I suggest that you stick to our original agreement and start selling your oil at, say, fifteen dollars a barrel as if it came from Grand Fenwick and continue to do so until we have gained our objective. At that price you will cut your losses in half. Remember our objective was to stabilize oil prices at some reasonable level and ensure continued and adequate world production."

"At fifteen dollars a barrel, I stand to lose thirty billion dollars—utterly unnecessarily," said Birelli. Mountjoy sighed. It was always the same. When some ivory-smooth and elegant plan had been arrived at by the unicorns for the saving of civilization, the lions started screaming about meat.

"You will not in the long run lose a cent," he said. "You may regard the whole of the Grand Fenwick reserve as yours, to be sold at cost of production plus a reasonable margin of profit. Let's see: twenty billion barrels at, say, fifteen dollars a barrel is three hundred billion dollars. What was that smaller sum you were talking about a little while ago?"

Over the long-distance line Mountjoy heard Birelli struggling to get his breath. Then he said in that same strangled whisper, "By God, Mountjoy, I've never met a man like you."

"There are few of us left indeed," said Mountjoy. "The important thing, as you know, is always to avoid being brought down by petty fears and anxieties."

Then he hung up.

CHAPTER

18

The news of the great Grand Fenwick oil strike was three weeks in being acknowledged by the world. The story was, of course, printed in the Grand Fenwick *Times*, sharing equal space with a rather nasty accident in which the wheel of a farm cart had come off, sped down the hill into the village, bounded over a stone wall, killed three geese and broken Ted Weathers' horse trough. Ted said the resulting ringing in his ears was so fierce he couldn't stand it and went off to the Grey Goose to apply the only remedy in which he put any faith.

Mountjoy was outraged at the oil strike's sharing equal space with an accident to a farm cart, but Stedforth, the editor of the paper and press secretary to Her Grace, said it was a matter of human interest.

"Sell more papers with cart wheels than you can with oil in these parts," he said. "This paper isn't *The Wall*

Street Journal, you know. Different areas, different interests."

Stedforth had actually worked on *The Wall Street Journal* as a junior reporter, and decided to return to Grand Fenwick because he couldn't switch his field of vision from wine, wool, weather and cart wheels to toothpaste, plastics, tungsten and ball bearings.

Stedforth did, however, send out a very good press release on the oil strike and he forwarded it, marked "Personal," to the anchor men on the media news telecasts. It arrived, unfortunately, on a day when the Mayor of New York, Lester M. Mercer, had announced that the city had been close to bankruptcy for two years, that the federal and state governments had refused any aid, and that he was negotiating with a group of Dutch bankers for the resale of Manhattan Island to Holland. On top of this a garden hose had been found dripping in the grounds of the nuclear power station at San Onofre, California, two geranium plants lay dead nearby, and there was talk of evacuating a large area of the Southern California coast including portions of San Diego and Los Angeles.

With these catastrophes gladdening the nation, the Grand Fenwick release was lost. But Stedforth remembered a friend on *The Wall Street Journal* and sent him personally a copy of the release.

"There's about twenty billion barrels of oil under this Duchy," he wrote. "I know it sounds fantastic, but so does driving an automobile around on the moon, and that's been done. Please run at least an item about it and send someone to investigate. One well is already producing a hundred barrels a day and fifteen more are to be drilled in the near future.

"The oil is being sold at cost plus ten dollars a barrel. It may sell for less. The object is to bring down world oil prices. Anybody buying Grand Fenwick oil at that price and selling it for more—at the current market price, for instance—will be cut off from supplies.

"How did you make out with that blond waitress in the coffee shop on Tenth Street?

Best, your old friend,

Bill."

Alas, Pete Martin, to whom the letter was addressed, was on vacation and didn't get it for two weeks. He did make a few inquiries, which aroused his interest, and then turned in an item on the Grand Fenwick oil strike to his city editor.

Students of history may be interested to read the small news item in *The Wall Street Journal* which announced to a busy world that one of the greatest oil strikes in the history of the planet had been made in Grand Fenwick.

It read:

THE MOUSE THAT POURED
Grand Fenwick Announces Vast
Oil Strike in Neglected Valley

"Following a survey by two eminent Swiss geologists, drilling for oil was recently commenced in an area known as Perne's Folly in the tiny Duchy of Grand Fenwick. In the face of worldwide disbelief, the two geologists insisted that there were oil-bearing marine strata under the pan of granite which is a geological feature of the area.

"The geologists, it is claimed, were proved right. After several weeks of drilling with diamond-headed bits, and at a depth of just over six thousand feet, oil of the highest quality was found. The reservoir is said to amount to twenty billion barrels, which would be enough oil to supply all the needs of the United States for close to three years at present rates of consumption.

"Of equal importance is the announcement of Grand Fenwick that they will put their oil on the world market at cost of production plus ten dollars a barrel in an effort to bring down world oil prices to a level at which neither industry nor the private consumer will be threatened.

"Further wells, it is said, are now being drilled in this field, which if the extent of the deposit is correct and the fiscal policy governing marketing is carried out would drastically affect world prices and supplies.

"Representatives of OPEC nations however, contacted by this reporter, laughed at this announcement.

"Mr. Alfonso Birelli, President of Transcontinental Enterprises and owner of Pentex Oil, who in the past has expressed deep concern over the oil crisis, has for a long time been a firm believer in the prospect of oil being discovered in Grand Fenwick.

"'We've knocked the top off the oil volcano,' he said. 'Now the artificial pressure will be released and business can go on as usual.'"

It was this story that finally made the world take notice. *The Wall Street Journal* was known to have a sense of humor but not on the subject of oil. Walter Cronkite put in a direct call to Grand Fenwick and having gotten as deeply embroiled with the telephone operator at Lyons as had Mountjoy finally reached the Count.

What Mountjoy told him, in calm and measured tones (having first inquired who he was), set Cronkite to calling

Birelli and soon the newshounds had the trail. The Grand Fenwick switchboard was so inundated with calls that soon all work on the rompers for the unborn niece or nephew of Elise had to be put aside. New York called, Paris, Los Angeles, called. So did Chicago, Pittsburgh, Philadelphia and Moscow. To that might be added London, Madrid, Caracas, Tehran (Mountjoy charmed the Ayatollah with his Persian but declined to open an embassy for Grand Fenwick in Iran), Qatar, Iraq, Saudi Arabia, Mexico City—in fact every part and portion of the world interested in oil production and sales called.

The telephone rang for hours and the questions were all the same. Was there really twenty billion barrels of oil in Grand Fenwick? Did the Duchy really intend to sell it at fifteen or so dollars a barrel below the world market price? And, these having been answered in the affirmative, was everybody in Grand Fenwick, including the Count of Mountjoy, mad? This was the only question to which a negative reply was given. In the end, it becoming quite impossible to have even a decent cup of tea without the telephone ringing all the time, Mountjoy went to the exchange and personally pulled out all the plugs.

"Let them sit and think about it," he said. "They've been long enough accepting the facts. Now let them stew for a while."

But they didn't stew for long. They acted. Cabled orders began to pour into the Duchy for cheap oil from such giants as Mobil, Texaco, Shell, Exxon, British Petroleum and others offering twenty and twenty-five dollars a barrel, which vexed Mountjoy enormously.

"This is the way big business is run?" he demanded. "We offer them oil at fifteen dollars a barrel or so, and they turn us down and offer twenty and twenty-five? In the world of business, it seems to me, nobody believes what anybody says."

Then came offers equally high, from the OPEC nations themselves; offers sent in cablegrams and offers delivered by personal envoys who having carefully consulted the maps of Europe chartered helicopters to arrive in the Duchy. Some, whose staff work was not up to scratch, arrived in Liechtenstein and San Marino, only to be told coldly that they were in the wrong countries.

But Mountjoy had at last gotten the attention of the world and with the cooperation of Birelli, who installed, staffed and personally paid for a hundred-line switchboard in the castle of Grand Fenwick, a conference of OPEC nations was finally arranged in the Duchy to last no more than a week and bring some order into what had now become a scene of economic chaos. Mountjoy insisted on a conference of but a week's duration. The problems of lodging and food supply would not permit longer debate and he quoted a saying of his father's that what cannot be settled in a week is probably beyond human agreement.

The Great Hall of the castle, occupying the whole lower floor of the donjon keep, was eminently suitable for the conference. The acoustics were marvelous. Microphones were scarcely needed and there was plenty of room not only for the delegates themselves but for their staffs who sat at ample tables behind them, tables which were soon filled with the reports, analyses, prophecies and dicta of the oil experts of every nation in the world, who included no fewer than five Nobel Prize winners.

Mountjoy insisted upon Gloriana presiding, and when she pleaded that she knew nothing whatever of the subject, he assured her that that was an enormous advantage which the others did not possess.

"Far too much is known or thought to be known about the oil dilemma," he said. "We are in a completely new situation and we must put aside all the learned rubbish which has been collected in the past and serves now largely to mislead our thinking. It is extraordinary how even intelligent men, of highest education, will refuse to accept that the knowledge they have accumulated, or think they have accumulated, is out of date. Your Grace, I can assure you that there is no one in the whole world better qualified to preside at this meeting than yourself, who, happily, know nothing whatever about it." He paused and added, softly, "In the unlikely event that you should be required to know or pretend to know something of the subject, I am here to assist you."

The first problem, of course, was to convince the delegates that the Grand Fenwick reservoir was of the extent of twenty billion barrels. Two days were spent on this, the geologists going over the echo soundings and the core samples and even asking for satellite surveys before, somewhat grumpily, they accepted the truth of the matter.

It appeared that at the time of the formation of the European Alps, the pressure of the tectonic plates had swept upward from the floor of the ocean and subjected to tremendous forces vast reefs of such an extent that the Australian Great Barrier Reef was but a minor marine construction by comparison. Not only that. By what Mountjoy called an act of God, all these marine formations had been deposited directly under Grand Fenwick, where over the eons the marine animal life had slowly changed into petroleum.

The whole deposit, then, lay under Grand Fenwick,

and its center being in the area of Perne's Folly, the deposit itself extended downward for upwards of a mile and perhaps more.

When all were convinced of this, Raoul de Verteuil, head of the French delegation, quietly mentioned that Perne's Folly belonged to a Frenchman, who had paid in full for the "possession, hold and use of the land and all things lying beneath it to be secured to him and his heirs and descendants in perpetuum." So the deed of sale read. The vast Grand Fenwick oil deposits, then, properly belonged to France, and Grand Fenwick had no right of any kind to their exploitation and use.

This really stumped Gloriana. She didn't know what to say and thought all was lost. There were smiles of relief all about the table, and several of the Arabian delegates, who had been buying deeply into United States banks with the profits from their huge oil sales, relaxed. Their heavy penetration and potential control of much of the United States economy could continue in the future. Freddie the Sheik, who was seated among them, and who had been wondering whether a man were really better off with a billion dollars than with a couple of million, gave her a little smile of friendship and encouragement, but that was all he could offer.

Birelli, after the French bombshell, dropped a glass of water on the table and although a silver stream of it poured onto his lap, he took no notice. He'd sold every asset he could to bring this scheme about. Now the whole plan was jeopardized by this damned Frenchman.

But Mountjoy was equal to the occasion.

He rose, adjusted his monocle, and looking directly at M. de Verteuil said, "Her Grace the Duchess is quite aware of the purchase in fourteen sixty-five of the area in

176

question by Gustave de Perne and I can assure the delegate from France that there is no intention on the part of the Duchy to abrogate that purchase agreement despite the fact that it is now over five hundred years old.

"The delegates present, from many nations of the world, will I think agree that any sovereign nation—and Grand Fenwick is a sovereign nation—is within its rights to seize foreign assets within its borders if this accords with national policy. Many examples can be produced to establish this right, and I think that a great many assets of Iran have recently been frozen by the United States of America, to quote but one example.

"In the case of the Duchy of Grand Fenwick, however, such a need is not present. Gustave de Perne was a man of eccentricity, brilliance and many gifts. Like Leonardo da Vinci, he never married and visited the Duchy only once in his lifetime, incognito and that for a period of two years. In that time he painted the ceiling of the room in which I sleep in a magnificent design of unicorns, lions and roses, and delegates may later wish to view that ceiling as one of the little-known treasures of Europe. I say he visited the Duchy incognito, having taken the name of Derek or Dennis of Pirenne. He died when that work was done in a scuffle with a knight of Vignon over a lady of quality (a married woman), by whom he had a child.

"That lady was Her Grace, Gloriana the First of Grand Fenwick. The details have in the interests of discretion been kept quiet to this moment, but they are fully documented in the secret archives of the Duchy, which I will now lay open to delegates. In short, ladies and gentlemen, the only living heir to the place which became known as Perne's Folly rather than Pirenne's Folly and the vast oil deposits which lie beneath it, is Her Grace, Gloriana the

Twelfth, now presiding at this meeting."

He turned in the startled silence that followed and said in an aside to Gloriana, "I beg your pardon for making public intimate details of your ancestry on such an occasion, but I trust Your Grace will realize that I had no other alternative."

"Bobo," whispered Gloriana, "is that another whopper?"

Mountjoy did not answer directly but said, "I can produce the needed documents to substantiate what I have stated," leaving Gloriana to wonder whether Mountjoy had not had these documents expertly forged prior to the conference in anticipation of just such a challenge from the French. "I trust it will comfort Your Grace to know," he added, "that de Pirenne was in every respect an artist, a mystic and a gentleman."

"What happened to the child?" asked Gloriana determined to press him on the subject. "Was it a boy or a girl?"

"A boy. It was brought up quietly in the monastery and, the legitimate heir being killed while hunting, the boy's name was changed to Fenwick at the age of ten, and he became the next duke." This accorded with Gloriana's knowledge of the history of Grand Fenwick, but with added details of which she had not been aware.

That settled the matter of title, though of course there were demands for documentation, all of which Mountjoy supplied willingly.

The conference went on for the week as planned. At the end, it was agreed by the OPEC nations (to whom Grand Fenwick was now added as a prominent member) that there would be an immediate reduction in crude oil prices to twenty dollars a barrel and continuing reductions thereafter as the Grand Fenwick supplies became increasingly available.

The experts now took over again and within a week were prophesying that the price of oil would level out at fifteen dollars a barrel, delivered to the refinery.

There was a curious, unlooked-for but very welcome side result. All over the world, people almost immediately became more cheerful. It wasn't just that the lines at the gas pumps had gone (people had gotten used to them anyway) and that oil for everything from heating homes to powering industry was assured in ample quantities. It was something deeper than that. It was a feeling that somehow or other even the greatest of problems could be solved and that humanity could trust itself both to get into enormous difficulties and get out of them again.

"It's like God didn't really intend us to come a cropper, but just to teach us all a lesson and get us to think again," said the landlord of the Grey Goose to the patrons of his barroom.

"I still got that bad pain in my head," said Ted Weathers. "I think I'd better have another glass of Pinot."

CHAPTER

19

A few weeks later, the Count of Mountjoy, enjoying what was for him one of the greatest of pleasures of life— a hot bath—with a copy of Tennyson's "Idylls of the King" propped on a special holder before him, was interrupted by his great-granddaughter Katherine strolling in upon him.

"My dear girl," said Mountjoy, glancing quickly downward and reaching for a large sponge, "you really must learn not to come in here without knocking. Privacy is part of a gentleman's privilege, whatever the modern teachings may be."

"I want you to come and watch my kite fly," said Katherine.

"When I've had my bath and my tea," replied Mountjoy.

"Could the tea wait? I'll scrub your back if you'll say yes."

"Oh, all right," said Mountjoy. "I suppose you'll want gooseberry jam?"

"Yes. You'll have to give me the sponge."

"That is out of the question. Use the scrub brush."

So she scrubbed his back—the Count loved that—and when he was properly dressed for kite-flying—he preferred a Donegal tweed and a shooting cap—he went out with her through the courtyard, she carrying the kite and he wondering why he could be coaxed into almost anything by a child of seven. He had a sharp need of a good cup of Grey's orange pekoe.

The kite was a blue one. When they got to an appropriate meadow Mountjoy looked it over and his heart leaped.

"You've forgotten the string," he said. "Let's go back and have tea. You shall have lots of toast with the gooseberry jam. Then we can fly the kite."

"It doesn't need string," said Katherine. "It's a stringless kite. Dr. Kokintz made it. It flies on bird water."

"It flies on what?"

"Bird water. I'll show you."

Attached to the bottom of the kite was a small plastic bottle with an opening at one end. The bottle contained a thick bluish liquid. Katherine held the kite in one hand and with the other put a whistle to her lips and blew a short blast. A note which Mountjoy recognized as that of a chaffinch was produced, and to his astonishment the kite slipped gently from Katherine's hand and mounted gracefully upward. It went up until it was just a tiny blue diamond against the sky and then glided down again, coming gently to rest in the long grass.

"Good gracious," cried Mountjoy. "What makes that thing fly?"

"I told you," said Katherine. "Bird water. Dr. Kokintz made it for me."

Forgetful of his promise of tea, toast and gooseberry jam, Mountjoy set off immediately to find the physicist, who was on his hands and knees in his laboratory watching a toy train, with twenty loaded carriages behind it, going around several hundred feet of endless track at a good clip.

"What the devil are you doing?" he demanded. And then, seeing no electrical hookup to the track, "How is that thing running?"

"Bird water," said Kokintz mildly, peering at him over the top of his rimless glasses, which had octagonal lenses.

This was too much for Mountjoy. He spotted a chair piled high with sheets of paper containing the eminent physicist's notes, swept them onto the floor and sat down.

"What," he demanded, "is bird water?"

"It's a new form of energy," said Kokintz. "Its basic components are ordinary water and glucose, which is a very common form of sugar. I got mine from a candy bar. But you can use fructose too. The atomic components are identical, though their arrangement isn't. And birdsong."

Mountjoy took a great lungful of air and blew it out through bellowing cheeks.

"You told me to work on a new form of energy. In view of the world oil crisis," said Kokintz. "And I did. It costs about ten dollars a hundred gallons. But with mass production the cost can be greatly lowered. In fact, it's an almost free form of energy. Like sunlight."

"Perhaps you would be kind enough to explain," said Mountjoy, holding his head in his hands. "Gently," he added.

He listened to the explanation but his mind was in a

whirl and in any case he wasn't interested in scientific details. Those details had something to do with methods of penetrating the atomic nucleus—by bombardment, by acceleration and by supersonic vibration.

"You understand that the forces which hold the nucleus together are immensely strong and when we are able to penetrate the nucleus by whatever means used, only a small portion of the force or mass is released. Also the results are random. Often we cannot accurately predict what particles of the nucleus are going to be expelled, or whether they are going to be split instead, forming new particles or portions only of the original particles," Kokintz said.

"Supersonic vibration as a means of atomic nucleus penetration has scarcely been tried to my knowledge and I wouldn't have considered it feasible myself except that I had a piece of Katherine's candy bar and I got interested in the sugars it contained and dissolved it in water. I am not going to go through all the steps which I took after-wards—if you're interested you'll find them in those notes on the floor. But the end product, produced after many steps including exposure to my white laser, was a bluish liquid entirely resistant to electrolysis which I thought might be of some use as an insulator in specialized hydro-electric installations. Then, while I was examining a small quantity of this inert water in a test tube, my chaffinches got hungry."

"Hang the chaffinches," said Mountjoy. "What happened next?"

"They started to chirp and the test tube of electrically inert fluid flew out of my hand and crashed against the wall of the laboratory. It was plain then that the liquid, which I have called bird water, contained an energy field resistant to electrical bombardment—or bombardment of any kind, as I subsequently discovered—but not to bombardment by ultrasonic sound waves emitted by chaffinches —bobolinks too, I believe.

"Subject to such a bombardment, not only do the molecules disintegrate but the atoms also, in a slow but steady release of energy. I can't claim all the credit. There's something about it in Tu-sin Yung's "Periods of Atomic Particles" and also Hazlitt's "Ultra-sonic Notes of European Wild Birds." I'll have to ensure that they get due credit when I put together my paper on the subject." He eyed the notes scattered over the floor ruefully. "I had a pretty good start right there," he said.

"Listen," said Mountjoy, "and please listen carefully. While you have been boiling up candy bars and playing bird concerts into the result, I have been working on the whole problem of energy for the Western world and indeed for the whole world. It is now solved—or securely on its way to solution. If you utter a single word about this wretched bird water, you will bring about the complete collapse of society as we know it today. You will produce mass unemployment. You will spread poverty throughout the earth. You will bring down the whole magnificent structure of capitalism in one terrible stroke. You will bring economic chaos to the whole of mankind."

"With bird water—free energy?" said Kokintz, amazed.

"Yes. With bird water. With free energy," said Mountjoy. "Free energy is the nightmare, the curse of the whole capitalistic system. Think, my good sir, for one moment, of the multitudes of people who are employed, directly or indirectly, in the gaining of oil from the earth. Think of the nations dependent upon it as their sole national asset. Think of the number employed in refining oil, in designing methods of refining and building refineries. Think of the multitudes building and manning ships to transport oil across the oceans of the world. Think of the people employed in factories manufacturing machines which will work off of oil energy—not just automobiles and farm equipment, but also airplanes and gas ranges and tires for automobiles, as well as gasoline stations and gasoline pumps—and horns and radios as well, I suppose. Think of all those people working away in what we blithely call the oil industry. Then abolish the oil industry and ask yourself what happens to them.

"Ask yourself also what happens to people who have invested their money in oil shares and all the industrial derivatives (including much of the plastics industry) of oil. Think of all these things and then think of the huge collapse when these jobs, these profits, these industries and all the commodities such as steel, copper, brass and even houses built by people who work in the oil industry —when all these things are gone.

"The world, in short, my dear doctor, would be destroyed by free energy. What the world needs is cheap energy but energy still affording a profit to the nations and people who produce, distribute and sell it.

"Think about all those things and then promise me solemnly that you will never breathe another word about bird water."

Kokintz looked at the train still circling the floor and at his notes scattered below the chair in which Mountjoy was seated. He looked at them for a long time and then he said, "Are you sure?"

"Yes," said Mountjoy. "I'm sure."

There was a fire burning in Kokintz's study and he slowly gathered up his papers, looked at them in regret, screwed them into a ball and threw them in it. Then he went to the cages where the chaffinches were housed and said sorrowfully, "We're too early, you and I. Too early. They are not ready for us."

A sudden and terrifying thought occurred to Mountjoy. "My God," he cried. "The Saudi Arabians. We gave them the Q-bomb to make them safe from the Soviet. But now that Grand Fenwick has all the oil needed to make the Saudi and other Persian Gulf fields not worth the risk of war, they don't need it and shouldn't have it."

"They haven't got it," said Kokintz. "It's over there." He pointed to a cupboard in the corner of his laboratory. "I gave them something that looked like the bomb but it doesn't have any insides. The instructions I wrote for unpacking it were so full of cautions about being utterly destroyed if they made the slightest miscalculation or slip that I'm sure that barrelful of wool and a useless bomb will remain in a temperature-controlled, vibration-proof room over there for ages and ages."

"Brilliant," said Mountjoy. "Deceptive but brilliant. The two go often hand in hand. The notion of a bomb rather than the bomb itself is all that is needed to make the Persian Gulf safe from outside aggression for many generations. I congratulate you."

He offered his hand and Kokintz took it. He was looking sadly at the little train bravely pulling its twenty loaded carriages around the endless track. It was beginning to slow down.

"Just a little while more?" he asked wistfully.

"All right," said Mountjoy. "But not a word to a soul." Kokintz gave the Count a whistle on which he blew a chirp. The chaffinches joined vigorously in. The little train speeded up and flew about the track. They both got down on their hands and knees to watch it, happy as boys.

After a little while, the Count remembered his promise and went to find his great-granddaughter to take her to tea. She handed Mountjoy the kite.

"I'm sick of it," she said. "It just does the same thing over and over again. It just goes up in the air and comes down again. The old ones with the string were better. More exciting. But I'd like a football and a doll."

"You shall have them both," said Mountjoy, taking the kite from her.

The tea was excellent and Katherine had four pieces of toast and gooseberry jam, which was more than was really good for her, but then, after all, it was a very special occasion, marking the celebration of the return of sanity and moderation to mankind.